Cambridge Elements ≡

Elements in Politics and Society in East Asia
edited by
Erin Aeran Chung
The Johns Hopkins University
Mary Alice Haddad
Wesleyan University
Benjamin L. Read
University of California, Santa Cruz

POLITICS OF THE NORTH KOREAN DIASPORA

Sheena Chestnut Greitens
University of Texas at Austin

CAMBRIDGE
UNIVERSITY PRESS

CAMBRIDGE
UNIVERSITY PRESS

Shaftesbury Road, Cambridge CB2 8EA, United Kingdom

One Liberty Plaza, 20th Floor, New York, NY 10006, USA

477 Williamstown Road, Port Melbourne, VIC 3207, Australia

314–321, 3rd Floor, Plot 3, Splendor Forum, Jasola District Centre, New Delhi – 110025, India

103 Penang Road, #05–06/07, Visioncrest Commercial, Singapore 238467

Cambridge University Press is part of Cambridge University Press & Assessment, a department of the University of Cambridge.

We share the University's mission to contribute to society through the pursuit of education, learning and research at the highest international levels of excellence.

www.cambridge.org
Information on this title: www.cambridge.org/9781009454537

DOI: 10.1017/9781009197267

First published 2023

A catalogue record for this publication is available from the British Library

ISBN 978-1-009-45453-7 Hardback
ISBN 978-1-009-19728-1 Paperback
ISSN 2632-7368 (online)
ISSN 2632-735X (print)

Cambridge University Press & Assessment has no responsibility for the persistence or accuracy of URLs for external or third-party internet websites referred to in this publication and does not guarantee that any content on such websites is, or will remain, accurate or appropriate.

Politics of the North Korean Diaspora

Elements in Politics and Society in East Asia

DOI: 10.1017/9781009197267
First published online: December 2023

Sheena Chestnut Greitens
University of Texas at Austin
Author for correspondence: Sheena Chestnut Greitens, sheena.greitens @austin.utexas.edu

Abstract: *Politics of the North Korean Diaspora* examines how authoritarian security concerns shape global diaspora politics. Empirically, it traces the recent emergence of a North Korean diaspora – a globally-dispersed population of North Korean émigrés – and argues that the non-democratic nature of the DPRK homeland regime fundamentally shapes diasporic politics. Pyongyang perceives the diaspora as a threat to regime security, and attempts to dissuade emigration, de-legitimate diasporic voices, and deter or disrupt diasporic political activity, including through extraterritorial violence and transnational repression. This, in turn, shapes the North Korean diaspora's perceptions of citizenship and patterns of diasporic political engagement: North Korean émigrés have internalized many host country norms, particularly the civil and participatory dimensions of democratic citizenship, and émigrés have played important roles in both host-country and global politics. This Element provides new empirical evidence on the North Korean diaspora; demonstrates that regime type is an important, understudied factor shaping transnational and diasporic politics; and contributes to our understanding of comparative authoritarianism's global impact.

Key words: North Korea, authoritarianism, diaspora, political behavior, human rights

ISBNs: 9781009454537 (HB), 9781009197281 (PB), 9781009197267 (OC)
ISSNs: 2632-7368 (online), 2632-735X (print)

Contents

1 Introduction: North Korea's Emerging Diaspora

This Element examines the emergence and significance of the North Korean diaspora. Over the past thirty years, a growing number of individuals have left the Democratic People's Republic of Korea (DPRK) and resettled in third countries, forming a new, globally dispersed population. North Korean emigration has been concentrated in South Korea, but not limited to it: while almost all DPRK émigrés initially settled in South Korea, a significant number have since sought asylum and resettlement beyond the Korean peninsula.

This specific form of migration, and the diasporic politics that it has engendered, has received little systematic attention. There is robust scholarship on earlier waves of migration that formed the Korean diaspora, including the diaspora's role in Korean state formation and contemporary transnational politics in and around the peninsula. The contemporary wave of migration from North Korea, however, is empirically distinct from previous waves, either those that preceded the modern Korean states on both halves of the peninsula, or the out-migration of Koreans from the peninsula's southern half since 1948. North Korean émigrés thus form the most recent layer of a broader Korean diaspora – embedded within global Korean communities, but also retaining distinctive identities and patterns of political behavior. As yet, however, there is relatively little scholarship on North Korean émigrés – their destinations, experiences, conceptions of identity, and political engagement, either in host countries or vis-à-vis their homeland. This Element systematically unpacks and addresses those questions.

As it does so, the Element also engages with the question of how homeland regime type shapes diasporic politics – a growing area of research at the intersection of comparative politics and international relations. North Korea falls in a subset of cases wherein the diaspora emerges from and engages with a homeland under authoritarian rule. Recent scholarship highlights that when authoritarian governments suppress opposition and contention at home, citizens can turn to migration and resettlement abroad to evade, organize around, and contest the power and control of homeland regimes. When that happens, diasporas become important sites of anti-regime activity; authoritarian regimes in turn strategically manage migration and diasporic policies to mitigate risks and control populations residing abroad (Ragazzi 2009; Betts and Jones 2016; Glasius 2018; Tsourapas 2018; Adamson 2020; Miller and Peters 2020).

The origins, political dynamics, and impact of these "defector diaspora" groups or subgroups, however, remain incompletely understood. How do waves of migrants fleeing authoritarian rule differ from and layer into preexisting ethnic diaspora populations, and what factors shape the form that these authoritarian diasporas take? When and how do these subgroups engage in political activity, either in the host countries where they resettle or transnationally vis-à-vis their authoritarian homelands? How do homeland authoritarian regimes view these diaspora populations, and seek to manage them to ensure that they don't become a threat? As one of the most closed nondemocratic regimes in the contemporary world, North Korea provides an important case study by which to examine these larger comparative questions.

Politics of the North Korean Diaspora explains the origins and shape of the North Korean diaspora, examines how North Korean émigrés' participation in democratic host countries intersects with their activism vis-à-vis the DPRK's authoritarian regime, and discusses how this approach to diasporic politics sheds light on comparative developments in authoritarian diasporas worldwide. The division of the Korean peninsula and subsequent contestation over migrant citizenship and asylum eligibility have generated a T-shaped diaspora, deeply concentrated in South Korea but with a thin, global distribution of diaspora members anchored in other countries. Many of these individuals left North Korea for economic as well as political reasons, and not all are politically active, but a significant subset engages in political advocacy in opposition to their homeland's authoritarian regime. They engage both *vertically*, as individuals or advocacy groups within specific host countries, and *horizontally*, as members of a transnational political community focused on a shared homeland; their global distribution has broadened the availability of external support and increased the effectiveness of both transnational and domestically focused advocacy efforts. In these efforts, North Koreans have acted as witnesses to North Korea's authoritarian past, as spokespeople for a people denied voice in the present, and as stakeholders in both their countries of resettlement and North Korea's political future.

Thus, the North Korean diaspora represents a fragmented, limited, but still significant source of transnational and pluralistic contentious politics, of a kind that is suppressed within the DPRK itself. The North Korean regime, for its part, appears to regard this nascent diaspora as a potential threat, and has taken steps to dissuade, discredit, and deter diaspora members from engaging in criticism and oppositional activity abroad. Thus, though it is small, the political significance of the North Korean diaspora affects both North Korea's political system and transnational global politics.

This section provides an overview of the North Korean diaspora, outlining migration processes and resettlement destinations. It argues for conceptualizing these émigrés within a diasporic framework: their global dispersion, distinctive shared identity, and emergent transnational ties qualify as a nascent diaspora. It argues that adding a regime-centered, *North* Korea–focused dimension to traditional primordialist conceptions of the diaspora sheds greater light on North Koreans' political identities, networks, and patterns of political action.

This allows us to assess the often-outsized impact émigrés have had on policy at a host-country and global level, and allows us to place North Korea in comparative dialogue with other diaspora populations from homelands under authoritarian rule.

Describing North Korean Migration and Resettlement

What – or whom – do we mean by "North Korean diaspora"? Empirically, two geographically overlapping but socially distinct networks comprise North Korea's overseas presence. One is chiefly composed of North Korean diplomats and overseas workers, organized in corporatist fashion and affiliated with the regime while posted abroad on behalf of the DPRK's economic and political purposes (Hastings 2016). The other network of North Koreans worldwide, however, is a more recent development: migrants, refugees, and defectors who have exited North Korea to seek a life elsewhere. I focus primarily on this second network, which has grown in size and influence even as the regime-affiliated network has come under significant pressure. Although the DPRK maintains a diplomatic presence in approximately fifty countries (East-West Center/NCNK 2019), UN sanctions and other international pressures have constricted and retrenched North Korea's regime-affiliated presence. As a result, the population of North Koreans around the world has shifted from regime-affiliated to increasingly oppositional.

Conventional wisdom on emigration from the DPRK usually portrays North Korean defectors and refugees as congregating in the Republic of Korea (ROK), with an undocumented, transitory population of unknown size in northeastern China. That perception remains largely accurate, although the population in China may have contracted during the global pandemic due to strict border and mobility controls on both sides of the China–DPRK border and post-pandemic repatriation efforts by the Chinese government (Yoon 2023). As of June 2023, an estimated 33,981 defectors had entered the ROK (MOU 2023) – by far the largest concentration of permanently resettled exiles outside DPRK territory.

Under the ethnic nationalist narrative framework articulated in both north and south, wherein both halves of the peninsula are part of a single Korean nation (Miyoshi-Jager 2003; Shin 2006; Grzelczyk 2014), this resettlement is not quite *diasporic* migration. North Koreans who migrate to South Korea ostensibly remain within a peninsular "homeland" – even though the southern half of this homeland has functioned as a separate country for over seventy years, and North Korean émigrés are separated from home, whether that home is defined as a *physical place* of origin, or in the sense of one's *family and community*. By contrast, a regime-centered notion of diaspora – focused on the commonality of

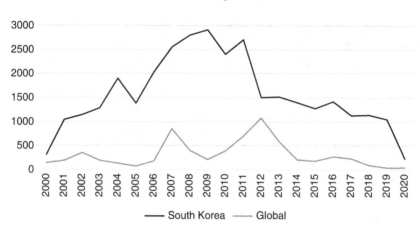

Figure 1 North Korean resettlement in South Korea and globally (2000–20)

emigration from territory controlled by the DPRK – captures this dislocation, and also allows us to place migration and resettlement to South Korea in a broader international and comparative context.

This shift matters because of late, an increasing number of North Korean emigrants have claimed asylum, sought refugee status, and attempted resettlement in countries apart from the ROK. North Korean onward migration from South Korea has also increased, making the ROK not just a resettlement destination, but a transit point in global migration chains – chains that originate inside North Korea, but no longer begin and end on the peninsula (Song 2015; Song and Bell 2019). Figure 1 compares resettlers arriving in South Korea to North Koreans applying for asylum worldwide.[1]

The UNHCR statistics shown in Figure 1 likely understate the size of the global North Korean diaspora, due to definition and measurement problems. For different reasons, China, Japan, and South Korea all avoid applying the labels "refugee" or "asylee" to North Korean escapees, so Japan and China are excluded from the "global" line. In addition, UNHCR has refused to make formal refugee determinations for North Koreans in Southeast Asia, due to the geopolitical complexities that having "two Koreas" poses for diplomatic relations and the option of simply sending such individuals to South Korea for resettlement (HanVoice 2016:5).

---

[1] Data on South Korea from ROK Ministry of Unification (www.unikorea.go.kr/eng_unikorea/rela tions/statistics/defectors). Global data uses "asylum applications" from UNHCR's Refugee Data Finder (www.unhcr.org/refugee-statistics/download/?url=5wmdYY). The UNHCR data excludes some countries, and North Koreans who initially claim asylum abroad could eventually resettle in South Korea, so the two categories depicted are neither exhaustive nor mutually exclusive.

Even where statistics are reported, neither asylum nor refugee numbers completely capture the North Korean émigré population. Not all asylum applications succeed; in Europe, there are years where countries rejected the majority of North Korean asylum claims (Section 3). In some cases, such as the Netherlands, North Korean asylees have resettled under Complementary Protections Status rather than as refugees (Burt 2015). Finally, UNHCR's "refugee" figure is the total DPRK-origin refugee population in-country, meaning that individuals enter that category each year, while others drop out due to naturalization, death, and onward migration. This makes estimates derived from UNHCR data uncertain, and best treated as a lower bound or baseline; these data showed North Koreans with refugee/asylee status in twenty-five different countries from 1990 to 2020 (Figure 2).[2]

Some countries (marked yellow on the colored version of Figure 2, or medium gray on the grayscale one) recorded only a handful of applicants in isolated years and none in others, suggesting cases of individual/small-group defection. These included Cambodia (1996/2007), Chile (2015), Finland (2020), Kenya (2019), Kuwait (2015/2016), Spain (2015), and Uzbekistan (1996). Others, like Israel (2013–20) and Kyrgyzstan (2006–10), show low numbers for a single stretch, and nothing afterwards. In other cases (red or darker-shaded in Figure 2), including the United Kingdom, Germany, Canada, and the United States, the numbers of individuals seeking asylum or obtaining refugee status are larger and remain consistent over years, suggesting more sustained patterns of migration and resettlement corroborated by journalistic or academic investigation. Section 3 of this Element assesses the factors that have shaped this global distribution.

There is presently little research on the global dimensions of the North Korean diaspora. A robust literature on the Korean diaspora concentrates primarily on historical processes of migration around and beyond the Korean peninsula (R. Kim 2008; J. Kim 2016; A. Park 2019), or on various forms of transnational Korean politics (N. Kim 2008; Chubb 2014; S. Y. Kim 2014; Lie 2014; H. O. Park 2015). A third strand of scholarship explores South Korean economic migration and ROK policy toward immigrants and the overseas Korean community (Park and Chang 2005; Lee 2010, 2012; Brubaker and

---

[2] These were: Australia, Belgium, Canada, Cambodia, Chile, Denmark, Finland, France, Germany, Ireland, Israel, Kenya, Kuwait, Kyrgyzstan, Luxembourg, the Netherlands, Norway, Russia, Spain, Sweden, Switzerland, Thailand, Uzbekistan, the United Kingdom, and the USA.

As of 2017, UNHCR recorded refugees/asylees in fourteen additional countries, but removed them later for reasons that are unclear: Angola, Austria, Costa Rica, Egypt, Hungary, Japan, Mexico, New Zealand, Philippines, Poland, Singapore, Turkey, Ukraine, and Yemen.

Dark shading (or red, in the color version) denotes refugee populations >25 for at least one year in this period. Medium gray (or yellow, if in color) denotes either a refugee population <25 for all years, or asylum claims without refugee resettlement.

Figure 2 North Korean refugees/asylees worldwide (1990–2020)

Significant resettlement

Isolated asylee claims or
small-scale resettlement

Created with mapchart.net

Kim 2011; Yoon 2012; Kim 2013; Mylonas 2013; Kim 2016; Lee and Chien 2017; Tsuda and Song 2019). For all its value, this work does not explain the role that members of the North Korean exile community have played in contemporary domestic and global politics. These outcomes become more apparent when we conceptualize a specific "wave" of migration, motivated by a desire to leave North Korea, that layers onto the preexisting diaspora, and that is embedded in larger patterns of Korean diasporic politics without being subsumed completely by them.

Research on North Korean émigré communities is unevenly distributed and almost exclusively composed of single host-country cases. There is extensive academic and policy work on North Korean resettlement in South Korea, including how North Koreans perceive and engage in the ROK's capitalist democratic system and on the challenges of effective resettlement and integration (Choo 2006; Lee 2016; S. Kim et al. 2017; Hur 2018, 2020; Denney, Green, and Ward 2019; Park 2023). Korean communities in Japan have also received in-depth ethnographic and anthropological attention. Other North Korean émigré communities, however, have been reported on solely by journalists (Canada) or largely overlooked (the Netherlands, etc.). This Element builds on existing work by drawing these case studies into comparative conversation, filling in empirical gaps, and treating North Korean émigrés as a network defined by shared homeland orientation – a significant, emergent form of transnational Korean mobility, identity, and political engagement.

A North Korean Diaspora? Regime Type in Diasporic Politics

Discussions of North Koreans who've left the DPRK immediately encounter difficulties of nomenclature, which shape political meaning, both in Korea and more generally (Chung 2008; Brubaker and Kim 2011). In South Korea, these individuals are *talbukja, saetomin*, or, officially, *bukhanitaljumin*;[3] English terms include *defectors, refugees, exiles, migrants, resettlers*, and *immigrants*. There debates over nomenclature reflect broader comparative conversations: Hamlin, for example, argues against reifying binary distinctions between migrants and refugees because such a choice implies, misleadingly, that motivations for border crossing are distinct, that refugees are needier, and that "true" refugees are rare (2021:6–18).

As an alternative, the use of "diaspora" can avoid some false binaries, treating North Koreans worldwide as a conceptual category organized by homeland of

---

[3] Overseas Koreans are referred to either by the homeland-oriented *gyopo*, or the more transnational and ethnically-oriented *dongpo* ("compatriots," but with a familial connotation). A North Korean defector's analysis of terminology appears in Lim and Zulawnik (2021:73–77).

origin, but composed of individuals and families with multiple motivations, levels of need, and types of engagement in political life.

A diasporic framework, however, does not resolve all definitional problems; the term remains contested and multivalent. The use of "diaspora" in this Element parallels Gamlen et al. (2017:511), who use the term to mean simply, "emigrants and their descendants." In contrast, Brubaker (2005:12) defines diasporas by subjective self-perception: "an idiom, a stance, a claim." Others combine objective and perceptual elements: Vertovec (2009:5) describes "an imagined community dispersed from a professed homeland" (see also Safran 1991:83). Betts and Jones define diasporas as "communities that are transnationally dispersed, resist assimilation, and have an ongoing homeland orientation," while reminding us that not all groups of exiles adopt a diasporic stance (2016:3–5). Adamson (2019) describes them as "constituted by a narrative of dispersion, attachment to a homeland, and a sense of group identity." Shain and Barth (2003:452) describe a diaspora as:

> A people with a common origin who reside, more or less on a permanent basis, outside the borders of their ethnic or religious homeland – whether that homeland is real or symbolic, independent or under foreign control. Diaspora members identify themselves, or are identified by others – inside and outside their homeland – as part of the homeland's national community.

In this sense, North Koreans beyond the Korean peninsula are a diaspora, at least an emergent one. They are dispersed from the homeland, whether that homeland is conceptualized as the Korean peninsula; as the country of North Korea; or as a specific local community of familial ancestry and origin. Many North Korean émigrés share a common sense of identity and even pride in their group, if not the regime that governs it (see Section 4 of this Element; Green and Denney 2021); they are recognized as North Koreans by others. They speak a dialect clearly distinguishable from South Korean, a difference that can condition migrants' network structure and patterns of political incorporation (Liu 2021). Many North Koreans share stronger within-network (bonding) ties than (bridging) ties to those outside; many have also formed transnational linkages based on their shared country of origin – particularly on anti-regime advocacy, and sometimes as a deliberate alternative to deepening ties with non–North Korean civic organizations in host countries (Bell 2013, 2016:265; Yeo and Chubb 2018:4). Indeed, the broader "North Korean diaspora" has within it a sizable "defector diaspora" engaged in political activism – though in North Korea's case, the activist subset is a comparatively large fraction of the whole (see Section 5).

At the same time, this transnational network of North Korean exiles is overlaid onto, and nested within, a larger Korean diaspora that emerged earlier, generated by different circumstances, timing, and processes. Cohen (1997) classifies diasporas into four types: victim/refugee; imperial/colonial; labor/ service; and trade/commerce. Much previous scholarship on the broader Korean diaspora has emphasized its colonial/postcolonial and economic dimensions.[4] North Koreans, however, hew closer to the victim/refugee type, meaning that specifically northern refugee diaspora threads are overlaid and woven into a broader, existing Korean postcolonial and labor-based/commercial diaspora.

This narrative is highly stylized; the North Korean diaspora itself is not monolithic, nor is the broader diaspora in which it is embedded. North Koreans in South Korea self-identify with the national community to varying degrees, and define that national community in a range of ways (Hur 2018). In the United Kingdom, identity perceptions stratify by age: younger North Koreans identify primarily as "foreign immigrants in a multicultural country," while older North Koreans are more likely to think in terms of membership in specifically Korean diaspora networks (Watson 2015). As Sections 4–5 show, however, this stylized narrative is useful for understanding how North Korean emigration and resettlement in areas where there is a preexisting Korean diaspora can *both* produce a separate diasporic layer with distinctive dynamics, *and* also generate new intra-diasporic cleavages along regime, language, and other lines for those who continue to define the diaspora with reference mostly to shared ethnicity. "Diaspora" is multivalent enough to allow fluidity: North Koreans are simultaneously members of a transnational network specific to North Korea, and members of a broader Korean community that has been dispersed by global forces of violence and development since the beginning of the twentieth century.

What, then, is the value of focusing more narrowly on the *North* Korean diaspora, and centering the authoritarian nature of the DPRK regime in that analysis? Omitting the nondemocratic nature of the homeland – in North Korea or generally – overlooks a significant factor that conditions emigration and resettlement processes; systematically alters the nature of political engagement with the homeland but also with host countries; and also alters the homeland government's calculations about diasporic policy. Ashwini Vasanthakumar (2022:22) notes that normatively, "exile is associated with unjust and undemocratic political orders." Empirically, recent scholarship has documented that authoritarianism differs from democracy systematically in terms of patterns of emigration permitted (Miller and Peters 2020); the diasporic management

---

[4] Transnationalism is deeply embedded in study of Korean identity and membership politics (Park 2005; Kim 2008; Kim 2011; Kim 2016).

policies that nondemocratic homeland regimes adopt (Delano and Gamlen 2014; Tsourapas 2018); the ways that citizens who grow up under authoritarianism perceive and engage in subsequent democratic politics (Pop-Eleches and Tucker 2017); and the strategies of political contention employed with respect to the homeland (Betts and Jones 2016). North Korean exiles, like exiles from other homelands, possess a kind of political and moral agency that challenges traditional notions of political community, membership, and obligation (Vasanthakumar 2022); they are not just witnesses to North Korea's authoritarian past and present, but representatives of its people in a world where the regime limits external voice and aspirant stakeholders in its political future.

In short, although authoritarian diasporas[5] share some features in common with diasporas from democracies, the opportunity structure and patterns of diasporic political action also differ in systematic and important ways.[6] This Element seeks to foreground these in its narrative, without losing sight of where and how diasporic activism might occur in the absence of homeland authoritarian rule.

Roadmap for the Element

The rest of the Element proceeds as follows. Section 2 begins with an overview of how the authoritarian regime in North Korea has attempted to control and manage its diaspora, historically and in the present. The regime's approach to diaspora management has shifted as state-sponsored, pro-regime groups no longer comprise the majority of North Koreans abroad, and oppositional voices have increasingly influenced the international community's policies toward the DPRK. Pyongyang dissuades emigration; discredits those who leave to domestic and international audiences; and attempts to deter and disrupt diasporic ability to engage in opposition and criticism. It employs domestic and international propaganda narratives about defection/re-defection; attempts to prevent linkages between defectors abroad and homeland residents; and threatens political violence, including assassination, to stop diaspora members from engaging in anti-regime political speech and action. Through these activities, the regime seeks to monopolize representation of the North Korean people abroad, countering and suppressing a "defector diaspora" that has increasingly contested the legitimacy of that monopolization (Ragazzi 2012). Extraterritorial discreditation and repressive violence also seek to confront emergent contention

---

[5] Here "authoritarian diaspora" means "a diaspora dispersed from a homeland presently governed by a non-democratic regime." This is distinct from Loxton and Power (2021; 465), who use the term to mean dispersion of former authoritarian regime officials within a country's political system.

[6] This was also true of South Korea under military-authoritarian rule, a point revisited in Section 6.

and opposition overseas, before it can infiltrate the homeland's borders, thereby bolstering regime security. These authoritarian efforts create the conditions under which North Korean diasporic politics emerge and evolve.

Section 3 asks where North Koreans who leave their authoritarian homeland resettle and why. What factors have shaped the global distribution of the North Korean diaspora? It suggests that contestation over citizenship in a divided Korea shapes global patterns of migration: although North Koreans meet legal and communitarian standards for citizenship in the ROK, actually claiming that citizenship in third countries during escape is arduous, and often contingent on geopolitical factors, which has complicated the North-to-South migration and resettlement pipeline. Additionally, many host-country immigration courts have interpreted Korean citizenship in ways that force reverse migration, reconcentrating North Korean émigrés on the Korean peninsula. The result is a T-shaped diaspora: heavily concentrated in South Korea, but with a broad, "thin" global distribution in a handful of countries that have either temporarily or indefinitely permitted small-scale North Korean resettlement.

Section 4 analyzes North Korean émigrés' political beliefs, especially about democratic citizenship. New survey data shows that North Koreans in the United States emphasize conceptions of democratic citizenship oriented toward civil liberties and rights, and have internalized many norms of democratic citizenship shared by American citizens. Survey data also suggest that for many North Koreans, pride in one's identity and exercise of rights as an American occur in parallel with strong remaining communal attachment to their ethnic homeland, indicating that civic patriotism and ethnic nationalism can be delinked.

Section 5 examines North Korean émigrés' political behavior. In general, North Koreans who have resettled in democracies show a high level of civic and political engagement. The T-shaped diaspora described in Section 3 also facilitates multilevel political action: members of the diaspora are often simultaneously engaged within their host countries and transnationally, and diasporic "anchors" in multiple countries have broadened access to external animators that have been critical to diasporic advocacy at both the domestic and international levels (Betts and Jones 2016). This structure has enabled the diaspora, despite its small size, to significantly influence host-country and international policy toward the Korean peninsula.

Section 6 assesses the implications of the Element's findings. It argues for a multilayered view of the diaspora, one that incorporates regime-specific forms of political identification and transnational opposition alongside historical and primordialist conceptions of diaspora. Placing the North Korean diasporic "wave" in comparative context, it argues that this Element's systematic incorporation of regime type sheds light on developments worldwide, from Hong Kong expatriates pursuing a "diasporic model of opposition" (Economist 2021) to advocacy efforts by Cubans in the United States to Svetlana Tikhanovskaya organizing an opposition movement from outside Belarus' borders. The section concludes by outlining questions for future research, such as how diasporas that emerge from authoritarian homelands change under democratization; how oppositional or "defector" diasporas relate to politically inactive or pro-regime diasporic subgroups; and what patterns of diasporic political activity stabilize or undermine homeland authoritarian rule.

2 North Korea's Diaspora Management Policies

The authoritarian nature of North Korea's homeland regime fundamentally structures and shapes diasporic politics. Pyongyang's approach to diaspora management, however, has evolved over time. For years, the DPRK relied on corporatist control and pro-regime propaganda to manage North Koreans overseas: exporting workers to (mostly) other autocracies/hybrid regimes in exchange for the economic benefits that such out-migration provided. As the proportion of the diaspora politically opposed to the regime increased, North Korea shifted tactics. Today, it seeks to *dissuade* most citizens from leaving; to *discredit* those who leave and voice criticism from abroad; and, using transnational repression, to *deter* and *disrupt* organized diasporic opposition.

Migrants are targets of "two kinds of policies: the emigration and diaspora policies of their countries of origin, and the immigration and immigrant policies of destination countries" (Muller-Funk 2019).[7] While almost all democracies allow relatively open out-migration, autocracies vary greatly in their approaches, with the DPRK on the most closed, restrictive side. Scholars suggest that autocracies must balance the economic benefits of emigration with risks to political stability. Emigration is a "mechanism of democratic diffusion" (Miller and Peters 2020:2); people "voting with their feet" can trigger mass exit and regime collapse, but even without that worst-case scenario, migration can create cross-border flows and "linkage" associated with greater likelihood of democratization (Hirschman 1993; Levitsky and Way 2010). Destination regime-type also matters: emigration to democracies is associated with greater likelihood of homeland regime transition, and diasporas have contributed to both anti-regime mobilization (Nedelcu 2019; Nugent and Siegel 2021; Esberg and Siegel 2023) and democratization (Levitt 1998; Camp 2003; Bermeo 2007; Chauvier and Mercier 2014; Kapur 2014; Mahmoud et al. 2017). Thus, even though most

---

[7] Until recently, comparative scholarship on immigration focused on wealthy democracies (Peters 2017).

emigration is economic, autocracies set emigration policies and manage diasporas with both economic incentives and the logic of political survival in mind.

North Korea is in many ways prototypical. The DPRK is highly restrictive of emigration, but allows it in select cases where perceived economic benefits are high. Pyongyang also appears to find migration to autocracies (especially China) less threatening than democracies (especially South Korea, but also the United States and the United Kingdom), consistent with concern about reverse diffusion of democratic ideas and mobilization from abroad. Accordingly, Pyongyang attempts to enmesh regime-sponsored (largely labor-focused) emigration within autocratic countries, where it can be regulated via corporatist control and pro-regime propaganda. To manage political risks, the regime dissuades out-migration altogether through border controls and by using "re-defectors" in state media; discredits those who defect in domestic and international outlets; and seeks to deter and disrupt potential opposition from engaging in anti-regime mobilization and activism abroad.

Corporatist Control and Pro-regime Propaganda

Before the 1990s, any North Korean abroad was almost certainly affiliated with the regime: diplomats, trading company representatives, or those associated with various "friendship associations." The DPRK's overseas presence typically operated along regime-led corporatist principles, in which "associational affiliations are structured, non-competitive, and vertical," existing in hierarchy rather than the diverse, competitive, and crosscutting associational forms that characterize pluralist systems (Gallagher 2020:4). Inside North Korea, as in other Leninist settings, organizational life forms a "transmission belt" between state and society (Lankov et al. 2012). Abroad, Pyongyang has applied similarly corporatist approaches: regime-sent diaspora groups are state-controlled and hierarchically organized to be responsive to regime directives.

Movement in and out of the DPRK is virtually forbidden unless sponsored and controlled by the regime; North Korea has generally sought to limit its overseas presence to situations or countries in which it could maintain corporatist control. Pyongyang's external revenue-earning endeavors, for example, relied heavily on diplomatic outposts and state trading companies, projecting a regime-led economic presence into the world that operated as an extension of domestic corporatist structures (Hastings 2016). State export of workers has been organized similarly: ministries, departments, or state-owned enterprises arrange and sign labor contracts that dispatch workers on tightly controlled overseas assignments where managers can isolate workers in specific housing, monitor their movements and interactions, and control the financial flows that their work generates (Arteburn 2018; Dept. of Treasury 2020). These temporary assignments are often in nondemocratic systems where DPRK political control is not objectionable to the host government. North Korea has also cultivated relations with a network of sympathetic "Korea Friendship Associations" or "Juche Idea Study Groups," generally Marxist or Communist in political orientation, establishing as many as 200 worldwide from the 1960s onward (Gauthier 2014; Dukalskis 2021:159–183; Young 2021; on pro-North Korea groups in the United States today, see Eberstadt and Peck 2023). While these organizations do not necessarily carry out diaspora management, they are examples of the party-led presence that Pyongyang has sought to project into the outside world.

This corporatist approach to diaspora management includes the pro-North Korea diasporic presence in Japan. In the mid-1950s, a pro-DPRK, left-leaning organization called Chongryon/Chosen Soren (General Federation of Korean Residents in Japan) was founded "under the direct control of North Korea" (Shipper 2010:60); fear of repression combined with connections to the DPRK helped channel Chongryon's political mobilization away from Japanese domestic politics, and toward support for Pyongyang as the legitimate government of an eventual, reunified Korean homeland (Ryang 1997, 2016; Lie 2008; Shipper 2010). Chongryon became a robust organization (more than Mindan, its weakly supported South Korea-aligned counterpart), maintaining hundreds of local branches, a press operation (including the *Choson Sinbo* newspaper), and a school system from primary level to a DPRK-funded university (Ryang and Lie 2009).

Over time, however, the pro-DPRK diaspora in Japan has proven difficult to sustain. Chongryon's involvement in the mass migration of 90,000 Koreans back to North Korea in the late 1950s–1960s began to corrode support for the DPRK, as returnees shared information about material deprivation and political repression in North Korea (Morris-Suzuki 2007; Bell 2018, 2021). Erosion of support accelerated with the granting of permanent resident status for Koreans in Japan in the 1980s, which facilitated travel between North Korea and Japan (Chung 2006; Ryang 2016). Government pressure after North Korea's nuclear tests and admission of abductions in the early 2000s led to further attrition and weakening of organizational ties to North Korea (Hastings 2016), what Ryang (2016:13) calls "a prolonged death for *Chongryun* as a mass organization of Korean expatriates in Japan."

Today, Chongryon's membership is estimated between 30,000 and 70,000, a fraction of its former strength (Bell 2019:32; Dukalskis 2021:171). Beyond numerical attrition, the pro-North Korean "homeland orientation" of Koreans in Japan has also declined, replaced by long-distance idealization without any practical desire to repatriate (Lie 2008; Shipper 2010, Bell 2018). Chongryon itself has shifted toward advocating for minority rights in Japan (M. Kim 2015; Dukalskis 2021:173–174; for examples, see *Choson Sinbo* 2015, 2018, 2019). For its part, Pyongyang has excoriated the Japanese government's "anti-Chongryon campaigns," and North Korean state media emphasizes Chongryon's support for the current DPRK leadership. The realization that Chongryon is "seemingly headed for accelerated irrelevance" (Dukalskis 2021:177), however, highlights the inadequacy of North Korea's attempts to maintain pro-regime diasporic orientation. In the face of fast-eroding support, Pyongyang has had to find new tactics for a diaspora increasingly composed of individuals opposed to the regime, and willing to voice that opposition and criticism from abroad.

Dissuasion: Preventing Defection

The first technique that North Korea has used to manage dissidence within the diaspora is dissuasion: physical border controls and information strategies aimed at reducing citizens' ability or willingness to leave.

Under Kim Jong Un, border security has tightened. According to Human Rights Watch, controls on movement within North Korea, and across the North Korea–China border, tightened after 2012 (Shim 2015). These numbers almost immediately impacted the flow of North Korean defectors arriving in South Korea, falling by half from 2011 to 2012 (Jung 2021). The COVID-19 pandemic intensified these measures further, as North Korea essentially closed its borders in January 2020 and has allowed little movement in or out since, even as trade with China – typically considered an economic lifeline for North Korea – dropped by over 90 percent. In August 2020, the Korean Workers' Party Politburo established restricted "buffer zones" along the Chinese border and demoted Minister of State Security Jong Kyong-thaek, supposedly for having failed to stop cross-border traffic (KCNA Watch 2020; M. S. Kim 2020; Weiser 2021).

These restrictions appear to have decimated migration out of North Korea, which relies on movement across the North Korea–China border and is heavily intertwined with cross-border market activity (Lee 2021). While much cross-border traffic is not intentional permanent defection, almost all defectors leave North Korea initially via China, meaning that border closures cut off the major exit points. Only 229 North Koreans entered the ROK in 2020, 63 in 2021, and 67 in 2022 (Jung 2021; MOU 2023). Though a lack of state medical capacity has limited the efficacy of DPRK controls for pandemic management and public health, these measures have nonetheless enhanced the state's control over markets and economic activity. Many North Korean entrepreneurs and market participants depended on trade with China to make money, so border closures will likely weaken their leverage and strengthen the state (Greitens and Katzeff Silberstein 2021), potentially limiting outbound migration for the medium to long term.

In addition to blocking outbound migration, North Korea also seeks to dissuade citizens from leaving by using testimony from "re-defectors": individuals who left for South Korea but then returned to the DPRK. Whether these individuals return to North Korea freely is unknown, and debated. ROK lawmakers have suggested that some individuals were tricked or "lured" into returning on false premises, or due to pressure on family members in the North (Harlan 2012; S. G. Park 2013). In 2021, South Korean authorities indicted a North Korean woman in the South for, as an Ministry of State Security agent, persuading other defectors to return to the DPRK (Yonhap 2021). Others have implied that re-defectors could have been spies who posed as defectors and then returned to generate credibility for regime propaganda (Lee 2013). A third perspective takes seriously the notion that defectors might find life in South Korea, and especially separation from loved ones, difficult enough to return of their own volition (J. M. Park 2013; McCurry 2014; Sunwoo 2014; Griffiths and Kwon 2017). After a spate of re-defector press conferences in North Korea, several additional defectors living in South Korea declared a desire to return (Haas 2018).

The total number of "re-defectors" is unknown. Around 700 (2.6 percent) North Korean resettlers in South Korea were unaccounted for in a 2015 study, but the majority were thought to have migrated onward, rather than having returned to the DPRK (Lankov 2020). The Ministry of Unification cited thirty re-defections from 2012 to the present; others estimate higher totals (Scarlatoiu et al. 2013; McCurry 2014). The last publicly known case of re-defection was on New Year's Day 2022, by a twenty-nine-year-old man who'd been in South Korea only fourteen months; before that, there were two re-defection attempts in 2020, one successful and one unsuccessful (Choe 2020; Kasulis 2020; Lee and Kim 2022). Of thirty people who returned north, at least six have defected again, returning to the South (Lankov 2020).

The North Korean regime employs televised press conferences with re-defectors to highlight its own ostensible benevolence. Prior to 2012, the regime had only publicized one re-defection: Yu Dae-jun in 2000, who returned to Seoul two years later (New York Times 2002; Cathcart et al. 2014:155). In Kim Jong Un's early years, however, Pyongyang held 7–8 additional press conferences, emphasizing the trickery, class division, discrimination, and poor treatment that defectors encountered in South Korea and contrasting that with the benevolence and generosity of North Korea's leadership (Gleason 2012; Kang

2014). The first two press conferences were in 2012; another half-dozen or so followed in 2013, usually with multiple re-defectors speaking at each. While public press conferences have declined since 2013, reporting as of 2018 indicated that re-defectors were making public-educational appearances in border areas to caution people against defection and to share their regret over leaving (Y. J. Kim 2018). This approach emphasizes the state's warm welcome of those who return, but also allows the regime to use citizens' voices to speak for the state, promoting the North's official narrative and criticizing South Korean political authority and culture at the same time.

Several themes in these press conferences augment the regime's dissuasion message. First, many speakers describe being tricked into leaving, by South Korean intelligence (KCNA 2012a; KCNA 2013a; KCNA 2013b) or "agents of the puppet government" of South Korea (Jin 2013; Kang 2014); brokers and "flesh traffickers" (KCNA 2012b; KCNA 2013a; KCNA 2013c); or greedy family members who'd already defected (KCNA 2013d). The allegation that defections are actually "abductions" done by dishonest ROK intelligence agents also appears in a 2016 CNN video, in which Will Ripley interviews the family of a woman who left for South Korea (CNN 2016).

A second theme is the difficulty of daily life and treatment of North Koreans as second-class citizens in a South Korean "society of darkness" (Jin 2013). The language is not simply that of economic struggle, though conferences do describe how "people like us have no money and cannot obtain work" (KCNA 2012a; KCNA 2013a). It is also an emotive language of cold-heartedness, rejection, and pain – "unbearable scorn and humiliation . . . [and] despair" (Jin 2013). Defectors describe being treated as "subhuman," finding it "hopeless . . . too painful to live" (KCNA 2012b; KCNA 2013b).

Bleak portrayals of life in the South are contrasted with Kim Jong Un's warmth and benevolence. In 2013, Kim appeared to set aside harsh punishments previously applied to those who attempted to leave; state media noted, "Thanks to the deep affection and generosity of Kim Jong Un, traitors can still live normal lives as long as they repent" (Kang 2014). Families of those who'd left for the South were asked to convey messages that returning defectors would be welcomed rather than punished (J. M. Park 2013). Press conferences echo this theme, often personally linking it to Kim Jong Un. In 2012, one of the earliest re-defectors said, "The dear respected Kim Jong Un did not blame me who did so many wrongs in the past, but brought me under his warm care. He showed profound loving care for me" (KCNA 2012a, quoted in Cathcart et al. 2014:156). Similarly, an article on the Laos 9 – nine young defectors apprehended in Laos and repatriated to the DPRK via China in 2013 – quoted another re-defector as saying, "Instead of blaming you for the path of treason, the motherland will engage you in a warm embrace and take care of you. Your past of crime will be erased" (Jin 2013). State media subsequently released footage of the Laos 9 in which they claimed to be content and patriotically loyal; one expressed a desire to join the military to "protect the Marshal [Kim Jong Un]," while another said he "should only trust the Marshal and follow that path [studying hard] to repay him" (Kang 2014b). Re-defectors typically do not just express gratitude for the regime's benevolence and mercy, but also signal redoubled loyalty and willingness to sacrifice for the North Korean regime and leadership.

Re-defector press conferences, then, appear aimed at several purposes and audiences. First is the dissuasive message for the domestic audience, which appears paramount: don't leave North Korea, because there is nothing in South Korea for you. Additional or secondary messaging, however, appears to be aimed (potentially) at North Koreans who've defected, urging them to confess and return to their homeland without fear of punishment. Re-defectors defend the regime against the threat that defection poses – if not directly to regime security itself, to the narrative of paternal protection and succor upon which the Kim family bases its legitimacy.

Discrediting: The Politics of Defector Legitimacy

Other propaganda seeks to discredit – to both domestic and international audiences – the accounts of those who leave and offer experiences and opinions critical of the DPRK. Discrediting is not always the sole purpose of the media segment in which it occurs; it is sometimes a moment in a larger narrative of rejection of life in South Korea and (re)-embrace of the North. One 2016 video of re-defector Son Ok-Sun, who returned after sixteen years, shows her tearfully ripping the cover from her memoir. She is shown visiting an amusement park and political monuments in Pyongyang, then a primary school where she embraces children dressed in traditional Korean clothes and speaks positively of the egalitarianism and welfare politics of North Korea (Rothwell 2016). A year later, state media featured Jeon Hye-sung, a woman who'd defected in 2014 and appeared on the popular TV show *Moranbong Club*, saying she'd been instructed to slander North Korea during media appearances (Hu 2016; Griffiths and Kwon 2017). While these segments are not direct attacks on the credibility of other memoirs or video appearances, they set up a presumption among the audience that such stories are untrustworthy.

Other attempts to discredit North Koreans who've left are more overt. For example, one KCNA piece characterized the landmark 2014 report by the United Nations Commission of Inquiry (UNCOI) on Human Rights in North

Korea, which was based largely on direct testimony from defectors (see Section 5), as "peppered with lies and fabrications, deliberately cooked up by such riff-raffs as those who defected from the DPRK and criminals who escaped after committing crimes" (KCNA 2014). Similar language appears in North Korea's communications to the United Nations and rhetoric in UN fora. A 2014 letter from Ambassador Ja Song Nam to the UN Security Council, for example, referred to the "human rights racket" as "hysteria kicked up by the human scum who fled to south Korea after having been forsaken by their kith and kin for all their evil doings and vices perpetrated in their hometowns. . . . a charade staged on the basis of misinformation provided by them" (Ja 2014). Another refers to the report as based on "fabricated stories" of criminals (UN WebTV 2014; see also comments by DPRK representative Kim Yong Ho, I. R. Kim 2016). At an unusual Council on Foreign Relations event in 2014, DPRK Ambassador Jang repeated his assertion that "so-called defectors fabricated their stories to raise up the price of their presentation" (Jang 2014). In 2015, a letter from North Korean Foreign Minister Ri Su-yong appeared to request names of those who'd testified before the UNCOI, saying, "we are ready to reveal to the whole world the true identities of each and every one of them and the crimes committed and the lies told by them one by one" (Anna 2015).

One revealing exchange at a UN forum, in October 2014, included two North Korean refugees who'd testified to the UNCOI. It reveals the centrality of defector voices in two respects – to the COI's legitimacy, and to the DPRK's efforts to undermine the legitimacy of defector speech and thereby the credibility of the report itself. A DPRK representative suggested that the Commission had used testimony "forced from witnesses by leading questions," a claim rebutted forcefully by the Commission's chair, Australian Justice Michael Kirby. The DPRK representative argued that the COI report had "no legitimacy" because it was "only based on the testimony of the defectors who escaped from the North after committing crimes" and that witnesses who left were unfair because they held "inveterate negative disposition against our political and social system." Kirby responded that allegations of criminality mean little when the very act of exit is itself considered a crime by the state – by definition, one cannot leave North Korea for the south and be anything else. The DPRK representative did not address two direct requests from Kirby to retract his allegation that witnesses were "human scum" bribed to appear (Kirby 2014). Kirby's affirmation of the credibility of the UNCOI's conclusions on crimes against humanity referenced the fact that every allegation was supported by direct evidence from testimony, while the DPRK representative's attempt to discredit the report suggested that witnesses were simultaneously coerced, dishonest, and biased.

DPRK state media rarely refers to individual defectors by name, preferring to collectively label them with emotive epithets such as "human scum" or "human trash" (*inkan suraegi*) (Fahy 2019). From January 2014 to May 2015 (the window around/after the UNCOI report release), North Korean media referenced human rights around a thousand times, using the collective label "human scum" 242 times, but only referring to individual defectors five times (Fahy 2019:209–211). A few particular individuals, however, are discredited by name, in great depth. North Korea has produced lengthy documentaries – often with English subtitles and available via Uriminzokkiri, a North Korea-affiliated press website in Japan – on high-profile defectors, presenting witnesses to their devious characters and supposedly criminal pasts. The documentaries only sometimes refute specific allegations of human rights violations made in defector testimony; at other times, they focus on overall character discreditation instead of refuting specific allegations (Fahy 2019:247).

Among the regime's targets have been Jeong Kwang Il/Jung Gwang Il, an activist involved in attempting to smuggle information into North Korea from the South; Shin Dong Hyuk, whose story *Escape from Camp 14* was one of the first defector memoirs published in English; and Yeonmi Park, a young female defector whose video testimony at a 2014 international conference catapulted her to international celebrity (Section 5).[8] One video on Shin, for example, argues that "[The US and ROK] are using the vicious 'defectors,' who ran away from the DPRK to escape the punishment for the crimes they have committed, to fabricate the human rights situation of the DPRK with preposterous false information. Sin Tong Hyok [sic] is at the forefront of this plot" ("Lie and Truth" 2014; Jin 2015). Shin's father provides alternative accounts for the scars on Shin's body (hot dog food spilling onto his back), the offense for which Shin's mother and brother were executed (murder versus political offense), and Shin's own role in reporting his family, while Shin's former mining coworker claims he hurt his finger after falling outside at night, and a neighbor alleges that he raped a thirteen-year-old girl.

In the cases of Shin Dong Hyuk and Yeonmi Park, Pyongyang exploited inconsistencies in their accounts to argue for general discreditation of defector testimony, and of any criticism of North Korea that employs defector testimony

---

[8] Park's speech: www.youtube.com/watch?v=Ei-gGvLWOZI. Over 200 memoirs by individuals who've left North Korea have been published in English and Korean; ~20 are in English, including those by Shin Dong Hyuk and Yeonmi Park (D.H. Shin 2012; Y.M. Park 2015). For a graph illustrating the growth of this genre, see Greitens 2021:123. Many of the DPRK's videos are no longer available, as YouTube removed Uriminzokkiri and several other North Korea-affiliated accounts in 2016–17.

as evidence. Shin's early versions of his memoir omitted a second camp where he'd lived for much of his life, described his escape to China differently, and left out his own role in the execution of his mother and brother. Shin told Blaine Harden, the journalist who'd helped him tell his story, that he found it too painful to recount some details, saying, "I made a compromise in my mind. I altered some details that I thought wouldn't matter. I didn't want to tell exactly what happened in order not to relive these painful moments all over again" (Harden 2015; Rauhala 2015). In Park's case, both Western observers and other defectors drew attention to inconsistencies in her story: the contrast between the tearful story of near-starvation told onstage in Dublin and her reputation for a relatively luxurious past life when she'd appeared on the South Korean television program *Now On My Way To Meet You*; what happened after her parents were imprisoned; who she escaped with; the narrative of her father's death (Jolley 2014; Power 2014; Vollers 2015). North Korea produced several documentaries accusing her of writing a "book of lies," building on these critiques (Fahy 2019:238–241).

The inconsistencies mattered in the public contest for credibility because this handful of defectors had become, as Harden stated about Shin, "the single most famous witness to North Korea's cruelty to its own people." Moreover, in Shin's case the story changed more than once; even Harden reluctantly noted, "Shin told me he is now determined to tell the truth. Regrettably, he has told me this before. It seems prudent to expect more revisions" (Harden 2015). Pyongyang's efforts to discredit Shin appear to have played an important role in his story's gradual excavation: it was Shin's father's appearance in a North Korean video that brought to light that he'd lived much of his life in Camp 18, rather than Camp 14. (Shin's father, in the video, denied living in a political prison camp at all, though the city he names would've been within Camp 18's borders then.) An amplification effect occurs: inconsistencies in defector stories create an opening for DPRK media to introduce an alternative narrative that amplifies those original inconsistencies and uses them to provide a picture of wholesale, irredeemable deception; these attacks, in turn, can heighten attention to the inconsistencies among external audiences, even sympathetic ones.

There is no easy way to assess how effective North Korea's efforts at discrediting have been. Some, including the American collaborators who helped both Shin and Park tell their stories in memoirs, note that fragmented, incomplete narratives are a mark of past trauma (Harden 2015; Vollers 2015; Fahy 2019). Others point, less sympathetically, to financial and celebrity incentives that predispose defectors toward sensationalism and exaggeration (Song 2015; Song and Denney 2019). As Haggard (2015) writes:

There are complex issues here, and they cannot simply be swept aside. The integrity of the legal process of which the COI could be a part rests on the testimony on which it draws. Facts cannot be treated casually. Memory plays tricks, but stories can also get told in a particular way and embellished: for psychological reasons, for opportunistic reasons, or for no clear reasons at all.

But the most important point is that the case against North Korea does not rest on the testimony of any one individual, but on the accumulated evidence from a variety of sources, from studies of the famine and survey of refugees we and others have done, to satellite imagery, to smuggled video footage, to the over-whelming weight of the refugee testimony on offer, now running to hundreds who had some experience with the penal system . . . . The core evidence is staggering.

Justice Kirby, the COI Chair, argued forcefully that "minor retractions of a single, highly traumatized person" should not overturn evidence provided by hundreds of witnesses at Commission hearings (Haggard 2015). Other advocates have likewise pointed out that changes to details in a handful of high-profile accounts do not discredit the much larger body of evidence that corroborates human rights abuses on a massive scale (Vollers 2015; Rauhala 2015). Their need to remind readers of this fact, however, reinforces the impact that North Korea's discrediting efforts have had on global conversation.

Deterrence and Disruption: Threats and Assassination

Pyongyang also uses extraterritorial repression to deter members of the diaspora from speaking about human rights abuses or engaging in oppositional activity from abroad. In this, North Korea is not alone; other states use transnational repression to silence critics and sever connections between dissidents inside and potential supporters or allies abroad (Tansey 2016; Glasius 2018; Adamson 2020; Dukalskis 2021).

In targeting the diaspora, North Korea seeks to limit information and money flows across its borders, perhaps out of fear that the role diasporas have played elsewhere – supporting opposition and sharing information that could catalyze protest – will repeat itself in the DPRK (Esberg and Siegel 2022; Nugent and Siegel 2023). Pyongyang limits reunions among family members separated for decades by the division of the peninsula; mail and phone calls to/from North Korea are prohibited or heavily monitored. From 1990 to 2018, the ROK recorded only 11,610 cases of letter exchanges; 1,755 face-to-face encounters involving 3,416 Koreans arranged by civil groups; and around 20,000 partici-pants in twenty-one government sponsored face-to-face reunions (H. J. Kim 2018); Korean-Americans are still excluded.[9] Informally, diaspora members

---

[9] In July 2021, after years of advocacy by Korean-Americans, the US House of Representatives passed two measures (H.R.826 and H.Res. 294) that direct the State Department to report on

use backchannels to call family and send remittances (Section 4) but risks vary over time, and a substantial cut of remittance money goes to brokers or bribing local officials (Greitens 2019), thereby siphoning off some of its potential for political empowerment.

Sometimes the North Korean regime employs rhetorical repression, wherein the state threatens diaspora members abroad with violence (Carter and Carter 2022). In the documentaries discussed earlier, for example, state media employs citizen voices to express anger and desire to do violence to those it accuses. Shin's uncle and the mother of the girl he's accused of raping express a desire to beat him to death ("Lie and Truth" 2014).[10] This use of citizens' voices – a technique that Fahy (2019:251) refers to as "the state as ventriloquist" – also appears in cases like that of Jang Song Thaek, whose execution was portrayed by KCNA as a carrying-out of popular anger and thirst for retribution (KCNA 2013e). In another state media article, re-defector Pak Jong Suk criticizes by name two activists involved in sending leaflets and USB drives to North Korea, Park Sang-hak and Kim Hong Gwang – the former of whom had been targeted for assassination a year earlier (I. B. Kim 2012).

In other cases, the regime's repressive activity toward extraterritorially based diasporic opposition occurs in cyberspace. High-profile, politically active defectors are commonly targeted by hacking campaigns (Kim and Weisensee 2021); many receive threatening phone calls meant to scare and intimidate (Jeong 2020). In 2018, hackers believed to be affiliated with North Korea obtained addresses and other information on almost 1,000 defectors from a database maintained by the Hana Foundation, the government body responsible for helping North Koreans transition to life in the South (Jeong 2018). Defectors in South Korea have alleged that some re-defectors returned to North Korea under direct threat of harm to family members who remain, a phenomenon that China scholars term "relational repression." In the words of one North Korean defector-activist, "North Korea used motherhood for a political purpose" by threatening a mother with harm to her son and his family if she did not repatriate (Harlan 2012).

A final tool that Pyongyang has used to manage opposition abroad is decapitation, a term used in security studies for targeted killing of an organization's leaders. Life as a high-ranking official is relatively dangerous *inside* North Korea, as the Kim regime commonly purges (sometimes executes) officials

---

efforts to find a way for 100,000 Korean-Americans to see family in North Korea before more of the older generation pass away. At the time of writing, the legislation is before the Senate Foreign Relations Committee (Chavez 2021).

[10] Interestingly, in part one of the same video, Shin's father notes the return of other defectors to their "homeland," and asks Shin to come home.

who fall from favor (Goldring 2021); a string of others have died in car accidents (Len 2003; *Dong-a Ilbo* 2013; AP 2015; BBC 2016) – a perplexing and suspicion-inducing pattern for a country with little road traffic. But North Korea's history of assassination efforts shows that its use of targeted political violence is not just an internal regime security strategy, but one that's been projected extraterritorially.

Some of the best-known assassination attempts outside DPRK territory were high-water marks of inter-Korean tension during the Cold War. In 1974, a North Korea sympathizer residing in Japan attempted to assassinate ROK President Park Chung Hee, instead killing Park's wife, Yuk Young-soo (Halloran 1974). In 1983, DPRK agents orchestrated a bombing in Rangoon (Yangon), Burma/Myanmar, that missed then-president Chun Doo Hwan but killed seventeen South Korean officials (BBC 1991). These incidents, and the bombing of Korean Air Flight 858 by North Korean agents in 1987, resulted in North Korea's placement on the US "State Sponsors of Terrorism" list. Two lower-profile events occurred after the Cold War, in the mid-1990s: in 1996, a South Korean diplomat was found dead in Vladivostok (Hockstader 1996), and in 1997, two men shot North Korean defector Lee Han-young in Bundang, a southern suburb of Seoul (AFP 1997; AP 1997).

After that, however, extraterritorial assassinations subsided for about a decade. In 2008, a North Korean woman was convicted by a South Korean court for planning to assassinate ROK officials with poison needles (Windrem et al. 2017). In January 2010, South Korean police arrested several individuals ostensibly affiliated with the DPRK's General Reconnaissance Bureau for plotting to kill Hwang Jang-yop, the highest-ranking individual ever to defect from North Korea (Al Jazeera 2010; Korea Times 2010). In September 2011, authorities arrested a defector, Ahn Hak-young, who allegedly planned to assassinate fellow defector and well-known dissident activist Park Sang-hak (the one mentioned by re-defectors the following summer) at a subway station in Seoul using a poisoned needle; a South Korean court convicted Ahn and sentenced him to four years' imprisonment in April 2012 (Park 2011; Feith 2013; Lim and Zulawnik 2021:120). The month before Ahn's arrest, in August 2011, two Korean missionaries working on the North Korea–China border were stabbed with poisoned implements two days apart, one in Dandong on the western edge of the border, and the other in Yanji, capital of Yanbian Korean Autonomous Prefecture, close to Mt. Paektu (Changbaishan in Chinese). The first man, Patrick Kim, did not survive, but the second, Gahng Ho-bin, did (Demick 2011a, 2011b; T. Kim 2017). Five years later, pastor Han Chung Ryeol was found dead with knife and axe wounds in Changbai county, also along the border (Choi 2016; Ryall 2017; Stanton 2016).

The most high-profile recent case was the assassination of Kim Jong Nam, eldest son of Kim Jong Il and half-brother of Kim Jong Un, who'd long lived overseas. In February 2017, two women approached Kim in the Kuala Lumpur airport and placed a cloth soaked in VX – a powerful nerve agent – against his face, resulting in his death en route from the airport to a hospital (Menon and Chow 2017; Windrem et al. 2017; Berlinger 2019; E. Kim 2020; Zolkepli 2020). Interpol issued a red notice for four North Korean suspects who'd reportedly been at the airport that day, but the individuals had already reached Pyongyang (BBC 2017). The two women (one from Vietnam, one from Indonesia) were tried for murder, but claimed to believe they'd been recruited to play a prank. Murder charges were dropped, and no North Koreans were charged despite widespread belief that the attack had been ordered by Kim Jong Un – either because an older half-brother could potentially be some kind of threat to Kim's leadership, or because Kim had become a source for American intelligence (Fifield 2019).

North Korea's assassination attempts are not always successful; the preceding data suggest that about half of known attempts fail. Most individuals targeted in the post–Cold War period appear to have been engaged not just in criticism, but in actual anti-regime activity – helping defectors escape, or holding a leadership role in a South Korea-based activist group. Extraterritorial assassination is a high-risk option in international politics, and comparatively speaking, North Korea employs it more often than the "average" authoritarian regime (Greitens et al. 2023), as it does with extraterritorial repression in general (Dukalskis 2021:72–73). Willingness to use assassination suggests the high importance that North Korea places on deterring or disrupting opposition activity organized by members of the diaspora that the regime perceives as a threat.

3 Shaping the North Korean Diaspora

Why have North Korean émigrés ended up in the places on the map in Section 1? While most global migration (90 percent) is driven by economic interests (Miller and Peters 2020:2), North Koreans report comparatively higher levels of political motivation for exiting the DPRK. North Koreans in South Korea cited economic livelihood as the primary reason for leaving (42 percent), closely followed by "political freedom" (37 percent), with family reunification (11 percent) and a better life for one's children (9 percent) after that (Hur 2018:103; see also Lim and Zulawnik 2021). North Koreans in the United States reported economic motivations at 42 percent, while 31 percent cited political freedom and 17 percent listed family reunification. Although migration scholars have long noted that political and economic motives cannot be neatly separated (Hamlin 2021), the distinctive nature of North Korean out-migration is worth noting. More North Koreans are engaged from the start in a "politics of exile" (Vasanthakumar 2022) than the typical global migrant, and North Korean authoritarianism has shaped the diaspora from its moment of birth.

An additional factor – contestation over citizenship – shapes the global distribution of the North Korean diaspora in two relatively unusual and cross-cutting ways. First, the practical difficulty of claiming South Korean citizenship during migration and resettlement contributes to emigrants' desire for onward/global migration; these difficulties are often conveyed and solutions identified via broker and local social networks in the process of choosing escape and migration routes (Greitens and Lee 2023). Second, however, legal contestation over citizenship and asylum status in third-country immigration courts has effectively channeled North Korean émigrés into South Korea whether émigrés desire to settle there or not. As in other cases, recipient countries selectively shape asylum policies and practices for geopolitical purposes (Abdelaaty 2021), and contested citizenship offers an opportunity for receiving countries to reject North Korean claims for asylum when they determine it is in their geopolitical interest. A T-shaped diaspora has resulted: a large community of émigrés in South Korea and a broad-but-thin distribution across other key countries.

Migration to and Resettlement in South Korea

As of mid-2023, nearly 34,000 North Koreans had resettled in South Korea. Conventional wisdom describes these individuals as having "automatic citizenship" in the ROK, and North Koreans do have strong claims to South Korean citizenship on both contractual-legal and communitarian-ethnic grounds. Legally, the ROK Constitution and Nationality Act (2010) together define North Koreans as South Korean citizens; Article 3 of the Constitution defines ROK territory as the "Korean peninsula and adjacent islands," while Article 2 of the Nationality Act extends citizenship at birth to anyone whose parents are ROK nationals or (if parentage is unknown) were born in the ROK. As a result, Koreans born in the territory claimed by South Korea, not only the territory presently controlled by its government, are defined as citizens under ROK law (C. Lee 2010, 2012).

North Koreans also meet typical standards for communitarian conceptions of membership, where ethnicity figures prominently. Ethnic nationalism is central to Korean citizenship; both states on the peninsula claim a singular Korean community defined by blood (*minjok*). South Korea's sense of ethnic community extends to the diaspora; like some countries in Europe, South Korea "selects by origin" in offering ethnic Koreans preferential basis for citizenship (Joppke 2005; Park and Chang 2005; N. H. Kim 2013; B. Kim 2019). Even within South Korea's hierarchical nationhood – where incorporation of co-ethnic immigrants varies by class, gender, perceived contribution to state developmental goals, and other markers – North Koreans retain privileged status compared to groups like *Chosonjok* (ethnic Koreans with PRC citizenship) or Soviet Koreans (Seol and Skrenty 2009; Chang 2012; Sohn and Lee 2012; Campbell 2016; Choo 2016; N. H. Kim 2016; Hundt et al. 2018; Draudt 2019). From the standpoint of law and practice, then, North Koreans are not "outside the state but inside the people" as Shain and Barth (2003:469) describe diasporas; they are, ostensibly, inside both.

The problem with this framework arises in the lived experiences of North Koreans who leave the DPRK to seek resettlement; it is not consistent with what scholars term "migrant-centered perspectives" on the migration and resettlement process. In practice, South Korean recognition of North Korean claims to citizenship is far from automatic. When North Koreans seek assistance from the ROK abroad, whether or not the government extends them the rights granted a South Korea–born citizen depends greatly on political context (Greitens 2021). In China, as well as in Southeast Asia, North Koreans seeking assistance have been turned away; escapee memoirs recall geopolitical considerations as the explicit justification offered at the time (for a fuller discussion of this dynamic, with examples from defector memoirs, see Greitens 2021:125–128).

China is perhaps the clearest case where the ROK's desire to maintain good relations with the PRC has prevented it from treating escaped North Koreans as full "South Korean" citizens. Not all North Koreans in China seek to leave permanently to resettle in South Korea, especially those in/around Yanbian Korean Ethnic Autonomous Prefecture in Jilin province, which is home to approximately two million ethnically Korean PRC citizens (*Chosonjok/Chaoxianzu*). Some North Koreans in northeastern China are state-dispatched laborers, while others cross on temporary work permits; still others are undocumented border-crossers seeking economic survival via participation in licit or illicit labor or women trafficked into areas with acute gender imbalances (Haggard and Noland 2011; Cathcart 2019; Greitens 2019). Especially in northern China, a significant number of North Koreans maintain close ties within North Korea, hold DPRK citizenship, and return to North Korea regularly. Others, however, who are trying to flee North Korea, have sought help from ROK facilities or government personnel and been rebuffed. The effect of North Koreans being unable to exercise their rights as theoretical ROK citizens in China is to obscure the underlying distribution of preferences among this population: we simply do not know how many North Koreans in China would choose to go to the ROK (or elsewhere) if given a choice, and are therefore trapped in the PRC involuntarily.

Under these conditions, the need to evade enforcement and repatriation is a major factor shaping the processes of North Korean migration. North Korean émigrés come from a highly censored, information-poor environment, which makes escapees heavily reliant on brokers and word-of-mouth information to decide when and how to leave, and what route to take (Greitens and Lee 2023). North Korea therefore confirms the importance of political information in migration (Holland and Peters 2020), but emphasizes that migration routes, not just destinations, are critical choices that affect individual outcomes and overall refugee flows and that information is often obtained by brokers and migration specialists, not migrants themselves. Traditionally, one key piece of information in this calculus has been where and how migrants can access a South Korean facility that will allow them to claim citizenship, and thereby secure the attendant right to enter the ROK for resettlement.

Even after émigrés physically arrive in South Korea, citizenship remains conditional. Arriving North Koreans are debriefed by a security team composed of military, police, and National Intelligence Service personnel, and spend three months at Hanawon (a resettlement education facility) before entering South Korean society. During screening and at Hanawon, many rights granted to ROK citizens are held in abeyance, though the ROK has reformed the process to extend more rights over time (Greitens 2021:128–131). Among other things, North Koreans must prove that they *are* North Koreans, not spies (see Section 2) or *Chosonjok* (who, as PRC citizens, are not entitled to ROK citizenship). Because North Koreans commonly arrive in South Korea without identity paperwork (which is dangerous to carry along most escape routes), they are "evidentiarily stateless" (Hunter 2019); they cannot claim the rights accorded to citizens until the state grants them citizen standing, and the primary form of documentation – a Resident Registration Card – is not accessible until one graduates from Hanawon (Greitens 2021:132). The requirement to prove one's identity to the state "inverts government by consent of the people into a regime of citizens' praying for privileges to be granted by permission of the government" (Sobel 2016:8).

Moreover, even if one establishes one's identity as authentically North Korean, the right to citizenship is not absolute, as the repatriation of two alleged criminals back to the DPRK in 2019 demonstrated (BBC 2019). To effectively claim the citizenship that they theoretically already possess, North Korean resettlers must resolve the state's security concerns. Unsurprisingly, many North Koreans perceive screening and resettlement education as tests, and citizenship as a status that is contingent, and only conditionally granted, if one can pass the state's tests (Greitens 2021:130).

North Koreans' experiences in South Korea influence the global diaspora by affecting whether North Koreans engage in secondary migration to other parts of the world. These experiences have changed as the defector/refugee population evolves. During the Cold War, North Korean defections occurred infrequently and defectors were often high-ranking officials perceived to have significant intelligence value; many were treated as anti-communist heroes, similar to defectors from the PRC to Taiwan during the same period (Chung 2008; Lee 2016; Morris 2022; see also Kim 2019; Chang 2020). In the mid-1990s, however, after economic crisis and famine swept North Korea, larger numbers of migrants began crossing into China and seeking resettlement in South Korea. These individuals were mainly women of lower socioeconomic status from the northeast, especially North/South Hamgyong – the area hardest-hit by famine, and from which travel to China was most feasible (Choo 2006; Eberstadt 2007; Chung 2008). Over time, these resettled North Koreans brought family members south, giving rise to chain migration and broker networks. The importance of economic survival and family reunification are reflected in the survey data cited at the start of this section.

Changing demographics correlated with shifting resettlement outcomes. Resettlers who arrived after 1994 tend to exhibit lower income levels, higher unemployment, and lower satisfaction with life in South Korea (Yoon 2001; Lankov 2006; Go 2014; Lee 2016). Since the mid-2000s, over 70 percent of arrivals have been women, many with children born in third countries like China. Until 2017, such children – who then made up over half of DPRK-heritage refugee youth in South Korea – were allowed to resettle, but remained ineligible for financial support (UniKorea 2017). Unemployment rates were high compared to South Korea's average (3.5–4 percent), though the percentage declined from 13.7 percent in 2009 to 7.7 percent in 2020; unavailability of childcare is a significant obstacle to finding work. Recently, these trends have improved somewhat: in 2018, 23.8 percent of North Korean resettlers received livelihood and welfare benefits, down from over 50 percent a decade earlier; job security and average monthly wages had increased (RFA 2019; see also Hana Foundation 2021).[11] Nonetheless, economic challenges remain significant.

Beyond economic livelihood, North Koreans often struggle to feel socially integrated into South Korean society. Starting at Hanawon, many experience "differential exclusion," wherein legal citizen status does not confer full social membership (Castles 1995; Y. Kim 2009; G. H. Song 2012; Bell 2013). North

---

[11] Hana Foundation, a government-funded organization that assists North Korean resettlers, publishes detailed annual data.

Koreans often come to South Korea with an expectation of community based on shared ethnicity (Nasr 2014; Hur 2018; Greitens 2021). South Korea's view of North Koreans, however, is one of duality: part of the community in ethnic terms, but outside and a potential threat in security terms; North Koreans are also regarded less favorably than other, more affluent migrant groups (Seol and Skrenty 2009; Sohn and Lee 2012; Son 2016). South Koreans sometimes speak of North Koreans as *gatjanhda*, or "not the same," and rates of both educational drop-out and suicide among North Korean resettlers are significantly higher than the South Korean average (J. Park 2023). Religious, civic, and pseudo-kinship network connections among North Koreans appear to be only partially successful in filling gaps left by social attitudes and state policy (J. Kim 2010; Cho and Kim 2011; Bell 2013; Han 2013). Memoirs by North Koreans express a range of simultaneous and contradictory feelings about their experiences: "guilt and appreciation, anger and sorrow, nostalgia and assimilation, hope and disappointment" (M. Kim 2013:523). Periodic crises among North Koreans in South Korea have drawn attention to these challenges and related policy failures, prompting changes to resettlement policy.

North Korean resettlers generally report satisfaction with life in South Korea (76.4 percent in the 2021 Hana Foundation survey). Nearly a quarter, however, have considered returning to the North.[12] The Ministry of Unification recorded twenty-nine actual re-defections between 2012 and 2019, though six subsequently returned to South Korea (Lankov 2020; see Section 2). Dissatisfaction, however, can impel *onward* rather than return migration, thereby contributing to the global diaspora population. One survey of North Korean émigrés in Britain found that secondary migration was motivated strongly by resettlers' perceived inability to access socio-economic upward mobility in South Korea, and a belief that these pathways would be more accessible abroad (Bell and Song 2018; Lim and Zulawnik 2021:221–222). Similarly, survey data from North Koreans in the United States found that resettlers emphasized their belief in greater opportunity in America, while also indicating the desire to avoid discrimination in South Korea. Out of fifty-two North Koreans in the United States who responded to the survey discussed in Sections 4 and 5, nineteen (36 percent) had been to South Korea before coming to the United States.

In short, the difficulty of claiming South Korean citizenship can "push" North Koreans to seek resettlement beyond the Korean peninsula. Because most North Koreans transit at least one additional country between China and South Korea (Greitens and Lee 2023), they can either migrate globally by going directly from third countries, if the opportunity arises during the escape process, or they can

---

[12] Because the survey did not ask them to specify the conditions under which they would consider returning north, this number is hard to interpret.

attempt secondary/onward migration from South Korea later. Certain countries also "pull" North Koreans, either because they have favorable immigration conditions or because they promise social/cultural capital via education and language fluency. These interlocking "push" and "pull" factors are augmented by increasingly globalized broker networks, which promise to help migrants find opportunity and mobility elsewhere, provide information on the relative benefits and challenges of different destinations, and assist migrants in navigating logistics and legal hurdles. In this sense, then, contestation over citizenship has contributed to global dispersion of the North Korean diaspora.

Contested Citizenship and Constraints on Diasporic Dispersion

Other facets of contestation over citizenship, however, constrain rather than facilitate global diasporic dispersion. Most important, the ROK's claim that North Koreans are actually South Korean citizens has fundamentally shaped the diaspora by precluding North Korean migrants from claiming asylee/refugee status in other countries and resettling there. Under Article 1(A)(2) of the UN Refugee Convention, individuals with dual citizenship must be in danger of persecution in both countries to qualify as refugees. Global immigration policy toward North Koreans, therefore, often depends on whether third-country courts rule that émigrés' purported South Korean citizenship makes them ineligible for refugee/asylee status elsewhere.

South Korea's own rhetoric on this matter has been inconsistent. Article 3 of the North Korean Refugees Protection and Settlement Support Act (NKRPSSA) suggests that protection applies to those who "have expressed their intention to be protected by the Republic of Korea," and in response to an inquiry from the British government, the ROK government stated that the "first and most important criterion" was "whether the person in question desires to live in the Republic of Korea … [protection] does not apply to those North Koreans who wish to seek asylum in a country other than the [ROK]" (UK *GP & Ors* 2014:24–25; UK *KK & Ors* 2011:11–12).

The NKRPSSA also specifies conditions under which protection/support may be denied or revoked; Articles 9 and 27 list offenses including drug trafficking, murder, terrorism, "disguised escape," intentional provision of "false information contrary to the interests of the [ROK] state," and attempts to return to the DPRK as grounds for ineligibility (ROK 2019). The ROK response to the UK stated that applications and asylum claims could be rejected if the individuals were "determined to be or have been spies, drug dealers, terrorists, or other serious criminals." In practice, as of 2019, approximately 280 North Koreans in South Korea had been granted citizenship but denied protection/benefits, usually because they failed to register by Article 7's deadline. In 2019, the South Korean government repatriated two North Korean fishermen back to the DPRK, against their will, without due legal process.

Despite this uncertainty, several foreign courts have ruled that availability of ROK citizenship renders North Koreans ineligible for refugee status. The United Kingdom's decision, for example, halted the growth of one of the largest North Korean émigré communities outside Asia, with an estimated 1,000 North Korean residents – most in New Malden on London's southwest outskirts (*Chosun Ilbo* 2011; UK ONS 2017). Early UK policy seemed only to exclude citizens who had first resettled in South Korea and actively availed themselves of ROK citizen status, as determined by fingerprint matching, a Readmission Agreement, and the addition of South Korea to a list of "Safe Countries of Origin" whose citizens were generally ineligible for asylum (Schwarzman 2008; Park et al. 2013; Wolman 2014; Bell and Song 2018). In several key rulings over the course of 2011–16, however, UK courts ruled that North Koreans acquire South Korean nationality at birth, making the Refugee Convention inapplicable and barring North Koreans from seeking asylum in the UK at all. This became "Country Guidance" for all future cases (UK *KK & Ors* 2011; UK Home Office 2016).

Even in the case of a North Korean husband and wife who the Court accepted had a "well-founded fear of persecution" and had never been to South Korea, whose two children were UK-born, the court determined that *"there is no group of persons whose only nationality is North Korean* .... these appellants are South Korean citizens and their asylum appeal must fail"* (UK *GP & Ors* 2014:3, 27–28, 33, 36). It thereby ordered their "repatriation" to a country in which they had never set foot.[13] The only exception made by UK courts has been for foster youth, noting the unreasonableness of sending them to South Korea without any familial or other support, though it observed that had they been adults, "return" to South Korea – a place they'd never been – would have been justified (UK 2015).

Courts in Canada, another significant site of North Korean resettlement, have ruled similarly. Starting in 2006, Canada processed an estimated 2,000 North Korean refugee claims.[14] Like UK courts, Canadian courts initially prohibited only those who had been to South Korea first (*Kim v. Canada* 2010; *Canada*

---

[13] The court also relied on the protection/citizenship distinction, noting that spies and so on might be denied protection or even prosecuted, but not repatriated; it ruled Article 9 provided grounds for withholding benefits, not citizenship itself (UK *GP and Ors* 2014:21–23, 28, 66). That ruling has not been revisited since the 2019 repatriation of two North Korean fishermen made clear that resettlement itself could also be withheld.

[14] Statistics available at Immigration and Refugee Board of Canada, Refugee Protection Claims Statistics: www.irb-cisr.gc.ca/Eng/RefClaDem/stats/Pages/index.aspx.

X(Re) 2015).[15] In 2016, however, Canada's Refugee Appeals Division ruled that even someone who had *not* gone to South Korea first was "a citizen of South Korea, and therefore does not require Canada's protection" (Canada IRBC 2016). The Canadian government began issuing deportation notices, which triggered a larger wave of self-deportations, while a smaller group appealed to stay on "humanitarian and compassionate" grounds (Young 2017; Al Jazeera 2018; Yoon 2018; Furey 2019).

Five years later, following an extended advocacy campaign by human rights organization HanVoice, the Ministry of Immigration, Refugees, and Citizenship Canada signed off on a two-year pilot program allowing HanVoice to resettle five families of "North Korean escapees in transit." South Korea's availability as a "durable solution" means that Canada will not *generally* accept North Korean refugees, but this program creates a special exception pathway available solely to escapees who've not yet availed themselves of South Korean citizenship (Rhee 2021). By the time the program was announced, however, advocates estimated that the total North Korean community in Canada had dropped to around 100 people (author's interviews 2018, 2021), and the regrowth allowed under the pilot program will be limited.

In creating a special legal exception for North Koreans who had not yet been to South Korea, Canada paralleled the statutory approach of the United States, which has accepted approximately 220 North Korean refugees under the 2004 North Korea Human Rights Act (NKHRA). Although in practice, some North Koreans arrived in the United States prior to 2004 (H. J. Park 2011), the NKHRA created a clear legal pathway for resettlement, stating that individuals from North Korea are eligible for refugee resettlement in the United States provided that they have not first resettled in South Korea and thereby already obtained ROK citizenship (Section 302(A)). This wording was a deliberate strategy by drafters to smooth over South Korean objections to the legislation, but courts initially interpreted the provision more broadly and ruled in 2006 to grant two North Koreans asylee status even though they had claimed citizenship in South Korea first (*Chosun Ilbo* 2006; Demick 2006; Gerson 2006; *Hankyoreh* 2006a, 2006b; KBS 2006). After some confusion – heightened by the fact that no North Koreans had actually made it to the United States from third countries via the NKHRA-specified process at the time[16] – the Board of Immigration Appeals issued a precedential decision in 2007, clarifying that applicants who accepted South Korean citizenship rendered themselves ineligible for asylum in the United States, but also specifically affirming that the *theoretical* availability

---

[15] In 2014–15, authorities discovered that many resettlers had not disclosed this on their initial applications.

[16] The first group to enter under the NKHRA did so in May 2006 from Southeast Asia.

of ROK citizenship would not make North Koreans ineligible, so long as they came directly to the United States (US BIA 2007).

North Korean refugees in the United States have been resettled in at least twenty different states through the nine "voluntary agencies" (VOLAGs) that handle all US refugee resettlements.[17] Numbers have remained small, due to a range of factors: relative unfamiliarity with the United States and the English language; the need to wait for months (or years) in third countries for completion of the State/Homeland Security screening process; and broader constraints on immigration due first to the Trump administration's immigration freeze and then the COVID-19 pandemic.[18] Despite this, however, North Koreans in the United States – both refugees and onward migrants – have become an influential community (see Sections 4–5).

Other countries have vacillated, creating small North Korean communities through slow and inconsistent legal processes. The Netherlands accepted a majority of asylum petitions in 2012, denied all 128 applications the following year, then granted one appeal on the basis of two arguments – that resettlement in South Korea would pose heightened risks to family still in North Korea and that South Korean citizenship was contingent rather than guaranteed (Netherlands 2014). It has also allowed some North Koreans to remain in-country under a more limited, non-refugee program, Complementary Protected Status (Burt 2015), while sending others to South Korea.[19] UN data and journalistic reporting documents additional small communities in Europe (Burt 2015; Power 2015; Levi 2017) and Australia (Jung et al. 2017). Japan also hosts several hundred North Korean emigrants, many of whom are individuals or descendants of those who left Japan for North Korea in previous decades and then returned (Ryang 1997; Ryang and Lie 2009). Beyond the core community in South Korea, the most significant diasporic communities are concentrated in liberal democracies in Asia, North America, and Europe – the T-shaped diaspora described in previous sections of the manuscript.

4 Citizenship and Political Belief

How do members of the North Korean diaspora think about political community and democracy? This section draws on an original survey of North Korean émigrés in the United States, informed by over a decade of discussion and

---

[17] US State Department data on refugee admissions and resettlement appear at www.wrapsnet.org/.

[18] In fact, part of HanVoice's argument for allowing resettlement in Canada was that US admissions/screening was so cumbersome and lengthy as to be practically unavailable (HanVoice 2016).

[19] Some deportations are due to government assessments that applicants are actually *Chaoxianzu/ Chosonjok*; it's unclear how many cases fall into this category (author's interview 2018).

interaction with, and participation observation of, communities of North Koreans in the United States; conversations with organizations focused on North Korean resettlement in South Korea, the United Kingdom, and the United States; and discussion with North Korea–focused advocacy organizations. The survey asked, in English and Korean, a mix of multiple-choice and open-ended questions where participants could provide qualitative detail. (For more detail on the survey, please see the Appendix.) The section also employs comparative data where available.[20]

Generally speaking, North Koreans in the United States hold conceptions of democratic citizenship similar to American citizens, suggesting strong internalization of many democratic norms. North Korean émigrés especially emphasize the importance of democracy's civil libertarian dimensions, though they weight scrutinizing or objecting to government actions as less important than "average" Americans. North Koreans in the United States also express pride in exercising the rights that come with (American) democratic citizenship, even as they retain strong communal attachments to their ethnic homeland – demonstrating that North Koreans can form strong notions of civic patriotism and civic attachment that are not dependent on ethnic nationalism. Given that the choice to leave North Korea is more strongly shaped by political factors than typical global migration (see Section 3), this section's findings about political identity and political belief may reflect a particular, selective "politics of exit" among those who have chosen to leave North Korea, or they may reflect an ongoing "politics of exile" among a group of North Koreans who retain an ongoing attachment to their authoritarian homeland while simultaneously acting as citizens of liberal democracies.

Political Community and Membership

How do North Korean émigrés think about political identity and political community? Scholarship on Korean nationalism emphasizes shared ethnicity across both halves of the peninsula, and stronger co-ethnic and communitarian conceptions of political community among North Koreans appear to facilitate integration in South Korea (Shin 2006; Hur 2018, 2020). For North Koreans in the United States, however, communal identification with the Korean *people* does not translate into political attachment to the Korean peninsula or the South Korean *state*.

When asked, "who do you consider 'your people'?" 29 percent of North Koreans in the United States gave some version of "all Koreans." Nineteen percent said

---

[20] Data on North Koreans in South Korea comes from the Hana Foundation (2021) survey unless otherwise stated.

"North Koreans"; 15 percent chose the narrower "North Koreans in the U.S.";
10 percent said "all Americans"; and only four percent said "Korean-Americans."
Notably, though the survey was administered in 2021, when reports of racially
motivated violence against Asian-Americans had increased, co-ethnic identification
does not appear to be driven by racial discrimination. In South Korea, 63 percent of
North Koreans indicated that they faced societal prejudice (Kim et al. 2017:29).[21]
Among US-based respondents, however, 48 percent reported not experiencing
discrimination at all, 33 percent had experienced it rarely, and 9.6 percent had
experienced it occasionally. Ten percent of those who did report discrimination
specified (in a voluntary, open-ended response) that it had come from other
Koreans, either South Koreans or Korean-Americans. Individual respondents perceived widely varying degrees of social distance from Americans: 21 percent said
they felt "very different," 29 percent said "somewhat different," another 29 percent
said "not that different," and 13.5 percent said "not different at all."

By contrast, when asked "What do you consider 'your country'?" the largest
group of respondents (54 percent) chose the United States, followed by another
15 percent who said "more than one country," usually then listing the United States
and North Korea. Only 6 percent listed "North Korea" and 7 percent "the Korean
peninsula." Many respondents, including those who listed the United States,
identified North Korea as a "homeland/hometown," while simultaneously expressing affinity with the United States as the place where they had been given equal
standing as a citizen and freedom to pursue their dreams. One respondent
explained, "The first country that gave me a passport to travel the world freely
was the United States. The United States is the country that provided me with
human rights and a foundation to live like a human being. The United States is the
country that protects and helps me." Thus, although Hur (2018, 2020) finds that
linkage between (ethnic) nation and state in South Korea facilitates North Korean
attachment/incorporation, North Koreans in the United States seem to hold a civic
democratic identity and civic attachment to the United States that is separate from
and coexists alongside their sense of ethnic community.

Similar patterns appear in a classic political identification question: "who
would you cheer for in a soccer match against North Korea?" Here, US-based
respondents exhibited a clear divergence in willingness to cheer for South
Korea versus the United States (Table 1). Many more North Koreans in the
United States opt to cheer (solely) for the United States than (solely) for South
Korea, while fewer respondents choose to cheer either for North Korea, or for
both. While this question does not fully capture the potential hybridity and

---

[21] Hana Foundation (2021) reports 18 percent of respondents experiencing discrimination/ignor-
ance; I cannot explain why two surveys in South Korea obtained such different numbers.

Table 1 "Soccer match" responses among North Koreans in the United States

Game	S. Korea	US	N. Korea	Both	Neither
N. Korea vs. S. Korea	13%		17%	52%	15%
N. Korea vs. US		54%	8%	31%	15%

ambiguity of diasporic identity, it is useful for purposes of comparability, and suggests that North Koreans in the United States feel a stronger active attachment to their host-country than to the southern half of their co-ethnic homeland, reconfirming the distinction between civic patriotism and ethnic nationalism.

Though not directly comparable, these data from the United States parallel findings from the United Kingdom, where younger immigrants of North Korean origin see themselves as "'foreigners' from two foreign states [the DPRK and ROK] living in a diaspora in a multicultural state" (Vertovec 2009; Watson 2015:547). Similarly, North Koreans in the United States describe themselves either as "American" (33 percent) or "an American from North Korea" (29 percent), rather than "Korean" (19 percent) or "Korean-American" (4 percent). Most define them-selves as coming from a homeland that is separate and distinct from that of (South) Korean-Americans, even though these two groups occupy overlapping (ethnic) diasporic space. In both quantitative and qualitative responses, US based North Korean respondents framed their origins and political identities as specific to *North Korea*, in tandem with expressing strong civic attachment to the United States. Migrant-centered perspectives captured in the survey data, then, provide empirical justification for treating the North Korean diaspora as embedded within but analyt-ically distinct from broader Korean diasporic politics, as explained in Section 1.

North Koreans express relatively high degrees of trust in the US government. When asked if they believed the United States would defend them equally as citizens, less than 8 percent said they "didn't really" trust the United States, compared to 52 percent who trusted "somewhat" and 35 percent who trusted the United States "totally." At the local level, 89 percent of respondents would report a robbery to the police, a number that matches or exceeds the range reported among Chinese diaspora in Eastern Europe (from approximately 60 percent in Bulgaria/Romania to approximately 90 percent in Hungary, Serbia, and Croatia; Liu 2021:70) and respondents in Israel (70–77 percent among Jews, 41–51 per-cent among non-Jews; Hasisi and Weisburd 2014; Nanes 2020).[22]

---

[22] Answers are not fully comparable since the Israel survey question asked about witnessing a robbery; questions to Chinese and North Korean migrants asked about reporting if the respondent was robbed.

Table 2 Composition of North Korean migrant social networks (US-based)

% Close contacts	Most	Over ½	About ½	Most not
From North Korea	15%	10%	27%	33%
Korean-American	25%	11.5%	25%	25%

Respondents who answered "no" to this question focused on instrumental reasoning, saying simply that they thought reporting to the police would be a hassle and unlikely to result in the return of stolen items; by contrast, respondents who answered "yes" explained their answer using both instrumental logic and the language of political trust, rights, and duties. They offered explanations such as, "I have faith the police will find the stolen things . . . it's the right thing to do and my civic duty for safety of community and myself . . . police and justice system exist for such reasons."[23] Paired with the data on dimensions of democratic citizenship (discussed later in this section), these responses suggest strong internalization of rule of law and other democratic norms.

How do North Koreans in the United States fare with respect to social integration and political incorporation? The distribution of US-based émigrés' social networks appears in Table 2. About one-third of North Koreans have mostly "bridging" networks (connections to people outside the North Korean community), while another third have primarily "bonding" (intra-community) networks, and the remainder are evenly divided between the two. If one redefines the network in ethnic terms ("Korean-American" rather than "North Korean"), then North Koreans in the United States tilt slightly more toward the "bonding" (intra-network) side.

Scholars debate whether strong intra-ethnic (or intra-community) networks facilitate or weaken the likelihood of integration. Liu (2021) finds that insular "bonding" patterns among linguistic networks of migrants are associated with lower political incorporation of Chinese diaspora members into European host countries, while Hur (2018) argues that strong co-ethnic identification can facilitate incorporation and participation among North Koreans in the coethnic context of South Korea. Our data do not suggest a strong prediction about which theory is right, though Section 5 shows that the network structure described here exists in a group that simultaneously exhibits relatively high levels of political participation.

Finally, how do North Koreans who've left the DPRK perceive North Korea? In contrast to many other diasporas, even those under authoritarian rule, North

---

[23] These responses are unlikely to reflect simple satisfaction with US government assistance, since 23 percent of respondents reported being dissatisfied with support provided by the US government (compared to 21 percent very satisfied and 50 percent somewhat satisfied).

Koreans abroad are highly constrained in communication with their family, friends, and communities of origin inside the DPRK. At the time the survey was administered in fall 2021, only 29 percent of US-based respondents had contacted someone in North Korea within the past year, and 27 percent had sent money/goods – meaning that about three-quarters had no contact with their homeland of origin. Pre-pandemic, 47 percent of North Koreans in South Korea contacted family regularly and 62 percent sent money, but the pandemic, as well as an overall tightening of social controls under Kim Jong Un, has limited both practices (VOA 2021). Most North Koreans in the United States report missing the "people and culture in North Korea" either very much (29 percent) or somewhat (44 percent). At the same time, however, émigrés distinguish between the people and the regime: most respondents report that they are not disturbed by criticisms of the DPRK government (60 percent say they are not disturbed at all, while 21 percent are not that upset, and only 6 percent are somewhat or very upset). These findings parallel Green and Denney (2021), who demonstrate that North Koreans have pride in North Korean culture much more than DPRK politics or ideology.

Asked about unification, North Koreans in the United States, like those in South Korea, uniformly thought it was important – but their reasoning varied. Thirty-three percent of respondents cited ethnic unity ("North and South are the same people"), while 23 percent chose "it is important for the North Korean people to also live well." Unification was perceived as important by 13.5 percent because it would reduce risks of war; 8 percent cited family reunification. Respondents in South Korea answered similarly: 35 percent cited ethnic sameness; 31 percent said "so North Korean residents can have a better life"; 15.8 percent mentioned separated families; 10 percent said it would "make Korea a more advanced country"; and 7 percent cited reduction in war risk (Kim et al. 2017:12).

Finally, when asked about the relationship between the United States and North Korea, respondent views varied widely. The most frequent response (23 percent) was "North Korea is a hostile threat," but 21 percent said it was "a country the U.S. should cooperate with." Seventeen percent said the United States should be wary, while 15 percent said the United States should help North Korea.

Democracy and Citizenship

What do North Koreans believe about democratic citizenship?[24] Classic work by Marshall (1964) treats citizenship and its attendant rights as *political* (the right to participate in one's government), as *civil* (the right to be protected from

---

[24] One complication in answering these questions is the diversity of views on how to define and measure democracy and democratic citizenship (see Schmitter and Karl 1991; Coppedge et al. 2011).

abuse at the hands of government), and as *socioeconomic* (the right to a government that provides for one's welfare).

Using this conception, North Koreans strongly emphasize democratic citizenship's civil dimensions. Sixty-nine percent said that the biggest responsibility of a democratic government was to allow people their rights and freedoms, whereas 8 percent emphasized participatory aspects (to give people a say in how government works) and 8 percent selected socioeconomic dimensions (to help people become economically secure). Similarly, when asked to rate the comparative importance of rights within a democracy, North Koreans ranked the right to be protected from abuse by those in power as most important (4.76/5), compared to the right to have a say in the rules or people that govern you (4.52/5) and then the right to receive help/welfare from the government (4.35/5).[25]

Survey data were not able to identify the underlying reason for this strong emphasis on civil conceptions of democratic citizenship. Several factors could contribute: individuals with a particularly strong emphasis on these beliefs may be inherently more likely to seek to exit the DPRK; direct experience with government repression may lead individuals to emphasize this conception over others; or the process of migration and resettlement may expose individuals to particular "rights discourses" where these concepts are emphasized. It is notable, however, that neither growing up in North Korea during the Arduous March period of severe economic deprivation, nor time in China, which emphasizes social citizenship and welfare rights over civil or participatory dimensions of citizenship (Perry 2008), appear to have led North Korean émigrés to emphasize the importance of these conceptions of citizenship over the civil dimension.

Other scholars disaggregate democratic citizenship differently, especially in the contemporary United States, where the survey's North Korean respondents were based. Goodman (2022) offers a tripartite conceptualization of the values associated with democratic citizenship that focuses on *behavior* (citizens who view actions like voting as important); liberal democratic *beliefs* (commitment to norms like tolerance and acceptance of diversity); and *belonging* (valuing indications of membership). Table 3 shows where North Koreans in the United States fall on a five-point scale on attributes of citizenship, using questions commonly asked in the International Social Survey Program and placed alongside Goodman's recent US baseline for comparability:

---

[25] No comparable survey data exists from South Korea or elsewhere for these questions. The closest is a 2016 ROK survey finding that 74.7 percent of North Koreans perceived income inequality as high, and 80 percent oppose reductions in poverty assistance programs (Kim et al. 2017:25–26).

Table 3 Dimensions of citizenship among North Koreans in the United States

How important is ___ for being a good citizen?	US baseline	Score	Difference
Obey laws and regulations	4.45	4.93	+0.48
Honestly file and pay taxes	n/a	4.89	
Understand people with other opinions	4.25	4.52	+0.27
Maintain friendship/ties with people with different opinions	3.95	4.04	+0.09
Accept people of different backgrounds	4.45	4.40	−0.05
Have patience when sometimes your side loses	4.25	4.38	+0.13
Understand how government and politics works	4.50	4.20	−0.30
Keep watch on government	4.50	3.53	−0.97
Vote in elections	4.55	4.59	+0.04
Participate in social/civic associations	3.40	3.41	−0.01
Speak English	3.85	4.39	+0.54
Feel American	4.05	4.13	+0.08
Help people worse off than yourself	4.25	4.47	+0.22
Protest/object when you disagree with government actions	4.10	3.49	−0.61
Support the actions of government	3.20	3.67	+0.47

These data suggest that North Koreans in the United States conceive of citizenship in ways that are broadly similar to "average" American citizens. Both groups value following the law (which researchers interpret as both respect for rule of law and compliance with authority), an interesting finding given the endemic nature of bribery in both North Korean society and the migration process (B.Y. Kim 2017). North Koreans in the United States also perceive formal participation and democratic *behavior* as very important (obey the law, pay taxes, vote, etc.), and they were almost twice as likely as North Koreans in South Korea to say that voting was a duty or responsibility (38 percent versus 20 percent; Hur 2018). US-based North Korean respondents do not think civic association is a particularly important conception of citizenship, mirroring both American and other post-communist citizens (Howard 2012). They value norms of toleration and mutual understanding (liberal *beliefs*), but place comparatively greater emphasis on *membership* (speaking English) than "average" Americans, a finding that Goodman (2022) notes appears across many immigrant groups.

Other results are more surprising. Despite the emphasis on civil liberties described earlier, North Koreans do not place strong emphasis on "oppositional" forms of political participation: they do not score "keep watch on government" as an important attribute of democratic citizenship (especially compared to the US baseline) and tend to view protesting/objecting to government actions that one disagrees with as less important than does the "average" American respondent. (Section 5 shows that this carries over into political behavior, as North Koreans in the United States tend to choose forms of political engagement other than protest participation.) Additionally, North Korean respondents reported believing that it is important as citizens to help others worse off than yourself, despite not ranking responsibility for socioeconomic welfare as highly as other government responsibilities; this seems to suggest that respondents view this as a social or communal obligation among citizens but not necessarily an important obligation of government.

Studies of post-communist (or post-socialist) citizens living in post-communist countries in Eastern Europe find that such individuals tend to be "on average, less supportive of democracy, less supportive of markets, and more supportive of state-provided social welfare" than citizens elsewhere, and argue that these views are more attributable to *growing up* in an authoritarian/socialist system than to *living (today) in* a post-socialist society (Pop-Eleches and Tucker 2017:1,105).[26] As diasporic resettlers who come from an authoritarian homeland to resettle in a liberal democracies, however, North Koreans are not entirely comparable. They themselves are post-authoritarian (and post-communist) citizens, but the societies they are resettling in are not, by and large, post-authoritarian or post-communist societies. The exception is South Korea, which is today a post-authoritarian democracy, but not a post-communist one, as South Korea's military-authoritarian period was characterized by strong anti-communist politics (Greitens 2016). Some of the survey data could be interpreted as corroboration for Pop-Eleches and Tucker's argument about the shaping force of growing up in an authoritarian/socialist system, but North Koreans in the United States, overall, appear to have more strongly internalized liberal and democratic norms than citizens in Europe's post-socialist countries. Future research could explore these questions more fully than existing data currently allow.

Finally, party identification among North Korean defectors/refugees in both the United States and the ROK skews conservative. In South Korea, almost half of North Korean defectors (48 percent) reported not identifying with a particular

---

[26] The authors use questions from World Values Survey rather than ISSP, so results are not directly comparable.

party, similar to the overall voting population in South Korea (Kim et al. 2017:33–34). Of those who did identify with a political party, however, 78 percent identified with the conservative Saenuri party, while 13 percent identified with the center-left Democratic/Minju party (for historical context, see Reidhead in Yeo and Chubb 2018). Voting behavior in South Korean elections is similar: 72 percent of *talbukmin* who voted in South Korea in 2016 chose Saenuri candidates, 18 percent Minju candidates, and 6 percent People's Party candidates.[27] Among North Koreans in the United States, 23 percent did not identify much with either party; 25 percent identified with both at times, and 19 percent opted not to answer.[28] Of the one-third who reported party identification, 18 percent identified with the Democratic Party, while 82 percent identified with Republicans (6 percent of the total sample versus 27 percent). Conventional wisdom about North Koreans leaning conservative, therefore, appears to be broadly accurate, perhaps reflecting the underlying emphasis on civil conceptions of citizenship documented earlier.

5 Citizenship and Political Behavior

How do members of the North Korean diaspora act, politically? While Section 4 sought to understand political *beliefs* across the diasporic community, this section focuses on political actions and behavior. In doing so, it shifts analytical focus from the broader "North Korean diaspora," composed of all émigrés from the DPRK, to a politically active "defector diaspora" subset. This distinction mirrors many diaspora communities worldwide, where between one-sixth and one-third of migrant communities typically engage in political action (Guarnizo, Portes, and Haller 2003). North Koreans are more politically engaged than this "average," perhaps reflecting the higher number of people who left the DPRK for political reasons and the community's view of behavioral aspects of democracy as particularly important (Goodman 2022).

In general, scholars find that various factors affect the level and focus of diasporic political engagement: diaspora size, cohesion, sustained communal

---

[27] For proportional representation, voting rates were lower (67 percent), but vote share similar: 68 percent Saenuri, 19 percent Minju, and 10 percent People's Party (compared to 26.7 percent and 25.3 percent from the overall ROK electorate). The April 2016 legislative elections were unusual in that the Minju party claimed a surprise plurality over the previously dominant Saenuri party, and a surprising number of seats were claimed by a new third party, the People's Party, which had been formed by Ahn Cheol-soo and others who had split from Minju earlier that year. National security and inter-Korean relations played a prominent (though not the only) role in the campaign, as Saenuri opposed reopening the Kaesong Industrial Complex while Minju favored it, and critics accused Blue House of publicizing high-level defections in mid-April in an attempt to sway voters (Ko 2016).

[28] This was an unusually high nonresponse rate, but appears to be primarily attributable to the presence of ROK citizens in the survey sample.

identity, immigration policy of host countries, host countries' foreign policies, and "the homeland legal/ideological approach to outside nationals" (Shain 1999:9–12). Scholars are divided, however, on how the characteristics of the North Korean diaspora – which is small, relatively concentrated, and sometimes fractious – should affect political engagement. Small, dispersed communities can struggle to forge cohesive identities, even with digital tools, and intra-diasporic cleavages can limit collective action potential (Shain 1999). However, if dispersion generates "bridging networks," it can facilitate host-country incorporation and widen political influence (Liu 2021). Below, I find that in the case of the North Korean diaspora, politically active "anchors" in key countries beyond the Korean peninsula have facilitated diasporic advocacy, and diversity within the diasporic network has provided more opportunities to collaborate with host-country animators, activists, and supporters, thereby generating new footholds for political action.

Political Engagement in Host Countries

North Koreans in both South Korea and the United States exhibit comparatively high levels of political engagement. The most recent survey of political participation in South Korea found that 70 percent of North Korean resettlers cast votes in 2016's legislative election, significantly above baseline voter turnout of 58 percent (Kim et al. 2017:33–34). Similarly, 70 percent of North Koreans eligible to vote in the United States in 2020 did, compared to overall turnout of approximately 66 percent, which itself was higher than usual for the United States electorate (Desilver 2021). This data is consistent with Goodman (2022), who finds that citizens who emphasize behavioral conceptions of democratic citizenship are more politically engaged.

North Koreans in the United States are also politically active beyond voting. Sixty-three percent reported having engaged in at least one of eight surveyed forms of political engagement (Table 4), notably higher than the global one-sixth to one-third baseline referenced earlier. The most common form of political engagement was speaking about North Korea to a civic organization, followed closely by volunteering and then by donating to a social/political cause (Table 4).

Some of the political participation and advocacy captured in Table 4 is a form of interest-group politics: advocating for policy changes toward North Koreans who reside in that country. This has occurred particularly in South Korea, the United States, and Canada. In other places, advocacy efforts by members of the North Korean diaspora have been more successful in altering the host-state's foreign policy toward the North Korean homeland than in changing policy

Table 4 Forms of political participation by North Koreans in the United States

Form of political participation	Percentage
Volunteered or given time to a social/political cause or issue	42%
Donated money to a social/political cause or issue	31%
Participated in a demonstration or protest	8%
Shared anything about politics online	19%
Contacted a politician or local official (city council, school board, etc.)	17%
Worked in a political organization	8%
Spoken about North Korea or your personal story to a civic, student, church, or other group	44%
Testified about North Korea or met with a government official to discuss policy toward North Korea	21%

toward migrant communities themselves: in Japan in 2006, for example, a DPJ lawmaker proposed institutionalizing assistance to resettlers, but the final LDP bill omitted this language, focusing instead on North Korea's abduction of Japanese citizens and broader human rights issues in North Korea (Arrington in Yeo and Chubb 2018:99–103).

In South Korea, stories about negative outcomes for North Korean defectors have sparked periodic campaigns for policy change. Outcry over repatriation of the Laos 9 in 2013, for example, led to establishment of a "National Community Overseas Cooperation Team" inside the Ministry of Foreign Affairs to standardize "protection and transfer of North Koreans"; further changes came via revisions to the NKRPSSA in 2019 (ROK 2013; Y. H. Park 2013). In 2014, following public scrutiny and claims about mistreatment, the government announced changes to the pre-Hanawon interrogation/screening process: renaming the Joint Interrogation Center "Defector Protection Center," ending closed-door interrogations, appointing a female attorney as human rights officer (*ingwon bohogwan*) and hiring more female attorneys, and providing human rights training to NIS employees (Yonhap 2014a, 2014b).

In 2019, public debate escalated again after defector Han Sung-ok and her six-year-old son were found dead in their apartment of apparent starvation. Han had left North Korea in 2007, was sold to a Korean-Chinese man in northern China, and struggled to care for her epileptic son after arriving in Seoul; media reported that she'd withdrawn the last 3860KRW ($3) from her bank account in May, two months before her body and that of her young son were found. The Ministry of Unification apologized and promised to close "blind spots in welfare" for defectors, while a coalition of activist groups has pressed for more systematic changes, such as increased childcare for the majority-female population, two-thirds of whom identify this as a major obstacle to employment and financial stability (Kim 2019; Kwon 2019).

Changes in presidential administration in South Korea have also typically been associated with changes in policies toward both North Korean defectors and inter-Korean relations. The Yoon administration has altered policy toward North Korean resettlers; pursued an increased emphasis on North Korean human rights by implementing provisions of a 2016 law that the Moon administration did not pursue; and announced its intent to investigate the repatriation of two North Korean fishermen in 2019, which was widely criticized by human rights advocates in South Korea and abroad (King 2022). In summer 2023, Yoon also announced a reorganization of the Ministry of Unification, which focuses both on inter-Korean relations and on support for defector resettlement (Ji 2023).

In the United States and Canada, major advocacy successes have, to date, centered primarily on codifying the right of North Koreans to resettle in-country at all. Human rights advocates began bringing North Korean defectors, many of whom were political prison camp survivors, from Seoul to Washington, DC, in the late 1990s to raise awareness of human rights issues in North Korea among policymakers and legislators. In 2003, around seventy of these individuals and organizations formed the North Korea Freedom Coalition (NKFC), which played an integral role in lobbying for the passage of the 2004 NKHRA, the legislation that opened a legal pathway to North Korean refugee resettlement in the United States (Section 3). After the NKHRA's passage, in 2005, President George W. Bush welcomed North Korean defector, author, and activist Kang Chol-Hwan to the Oval Office as a visible symbol of support for North Korean human rights (Lim and Zulawnik 2021:25).[29] Once North Koreans could legally enter the United States, many became involved in further advocacy efforts related to North Korea, as evidenced by the 21 percent of survey respondents who say they have met with legislators or policymakers.

In Canada, advocacy efforts eventually resulted in the 2021 announcement of a Special Policy Program under Section 25(2) of Canada's Immigration and Refugee Protection Act,[30] which allowed Toronto-based organization HanVoice to resettle five North Korean families during a two-year pilot. Over eight years, advocates met with Immigration Ministers across Conservative and

---

[29] https://georgewbush-whitehouse.archives.gov/news/releases/2005/06/images/20050613-1_p45011-005-515h.html

[30] This exemption has been used before for stateless Vietnamese in Southeast Asia and Tibetans in India (HanVoice 2016:6).

Liberal governments; organized lobbying days for grassroots volunteers from across Canada to meet in Ottawa with parliamentarians/policymakers; testified in six hearings before the House of Commons and Senate; and worked to generate media attention (HanVoice 2021). Advocates also deliberately focused their proposals on assisting North Korean women and children, drawing attention to the prevalence of sexual/gender-based violence during migration, in hopes that the appeal to protect a vulnerable, majority-female population would resonate with the Trudeau government's emphasis on feminist foreign policy (author's interview 2021). However, because these efforts sought to alter an existing government decision to vacate many North Korean residents' status, North Korean diaspora members in Canada were potentially vulnerable to deportation during the time this advocacy was occurring. As a result, advocates followed the older US model of bringing defectors from South Korea to testify, and a Canadian permanent resident, Sam, served as the "face" of the campaign to avoid involving those vulnerable to status challenges and deportation in potentially risky activism (author's interview 2021).[31] This story reflects broader themes of this Element: the constraints that legal contestation over citizenship puts on diasporic growth and impact, but also the effect that even a small number of diasporic "anchors," working in collaboration with host-country supporters, can ultimately have on policy.

Unlike Canada's pilot program, the United States and Japan do not allow private sponsorship of refugees; these two countries' government support programs for North Korean resettlement are also much more limited than South Korea's. In both countries, therefore, resettlement support and integration work falls largely to civil society. US refugee programs are run by nine VOLAGs, which resettle refugees from around the world. After the short period of formal VOLAG-managed assistance, however, additional help is sometimes provided by North Korea–specific organizations (J. I. Kim 2010). Among these groups are organizations whose primary focus is on human rights in the DPRK itself: Liberty in North Korea (LINK), the Committee on Human Rights in North Korea (HRNK), NKFC, and Lumen. Others offer programs specifically for US-based North Korean refugees: ENOK/Empower House, a residential program in Chicago focused on English-language proficiency (author's interview 2017); faith-based Durihana-USA, which focuses on US resettlement, while its sister ministry Durihana (with offices in both the United States and South Korea) focuses on North Korea issues; the George W. Bush Institute, which funds scholarships for North Korean refugees in the United States (Bush Center 2014, 2019; Lloyd 2019); and an organization called NKinUSA,

---

[31] www.youtube.com/watch?v=urP4kvbsXQ0

founded and led by North Korean refugee sisters Jinhye and Grace Jo, which merged with Empower House/ENOK in late 2018. Only 28 percent of North Koreans in the United States, however, report receiving assistance from organizations other than the government. Korea-specific organizations and churches express frustration that resettlement processes do not allow them to be matched with North Korean refugees that they are especially equipped and motivated to help (author's interviews 2017, 2018).[32]

In Japan, assistance to "returnees" (a term used because North Koreans must show a preexisting connection to Japan to enter, or "return," there) is similarly dispersed across a number of organizations, many of whom also do other, overlapping work. These include repatriate-focused Mamorukai; an organization called Life Funds for North Korean Refugees (LFKNR) that split from Mamorukai in 1998; an Escapee Assistance Office in Mindan (the pro-ROK counterpart-organization to Chosen Soren); and an escapee association known as Modu Moija, or Korea of All, which formed after the COI in 2014 to draw attention to escapees in Japan and to call for repatriation of additional Koreans back from North Korea (Arrington in Yeo and Chubb 2018:94–99; Kim 2012; Bell 2016). LFNKR assists with both escape and resettlement, while Mamorukai and Mindan focus only on post-arrival resettlement assistance; both Modu Moija and LFNKR also participate in transnational advocacy.

In Japan, as in other countries, the dispersion of the diaspora across numerous organizations is both a strength and weakness. Organizational pluralism prevents any single organization from aggregating all voices and perspectives and can limit coordination and concentration of effort at times when that might be useful for policy impact. Over the long term, however, this diversity and pluralism also contribute to diversification and breadth of the diaspora's support networks and activities, which can widen the opportunity structure for activism and, over time, increase political impact.

Transnational Advocacy and Activism

Members of the North Korean diaspora have played an integral role in transnational advocacy, particularly on human rights in North Korea. The T-shaped diaspora, and presence of diasporic "anchors" in key countries, has facilitated transnational political action, allowing the diasporic community to substitute for domestic civil society in international fora (Yeo and Chubb 2018).

---

[32] A US government official cited privacy, feasibility, and fairness across refugee groups as reasons (author's interview 2018). The barriers between Korean or Korean-American associations and refugee resettlement processes may contribute to North Koreans' perception of an identity that is distinct from Korean-Americans.

Somewhat contrary to conventional wisdom, North Korean émigrés' organizational fragmentation and diversity of anchors has allowed the diaspora, as a whole, to connect with a wider range of external "animators" in host countries over time, broadening political support. The relationship between host-country and transnational advocacy is not one-way, however; in some important cases, transnational activism has also been a stepping-stone to larger roles for diaspora members in host-country domestic politics.

In both South Korea and the United States, influential North Korea–related advocacy organizations emerged in the mid-1990s, as the diaspora was beginning to grow. In 1996, Benjamin Hyun Yoon, a long-time advocate for political prisoners in South Korea, founded Citizens' Alliance to Help Political Prisoners in North Korea.[33] Hosaniak (in Yeo and Chubb 2018:132) writes that Yoon decided to pursue a transnational advocacy strategy because of the "constrained advocacy space" in South Korea, in which the issue of North Korean human rights had been "captured" by conservative actors and was unable to gain much progressive support. Yoon aimed to "amplify victim's voices beyond the South Korean context," and by fall 1996, Citizens' Alliance was publishing testimonies from North Korean defectors for distribution to an international audience (Hosaniak in Yeo and Chubb 2018:134). In 1999, the organization convened its first international conference in Seoul, bringing together eight organizations from five countries, and subsequently rotated conference locations around the world – Prague (where escapees met with Vaclav Havel), Poland, Norway, the United Kingdom, Australia, Canada, Switzerland, Indonesia, and Germany – in an effort to build bases of support for North Korea human rights advocacy in each place (Hosaniak in Yeo and Chubb 2018:135).

In the late 1990s, the Defense Forum Foundation (DFF) – a US-based organization with a Reagan-esque orientation toward freedom and national defense – began inviting North Korean defectors, particularly political prison camp survivors, to come to the United States to speak to and meet with legislators. DFF founder Suzanne Scholte characterizes this as "probably the most important step" DFF took during that period (author's interview 2017); in 2003, DFF played a major role in forming the NKFC, the umbrella group of around seventy individuals and organizations described earlier. Just prior to that, in 2001, an organization called the Committee for Human Rights in North Korea (HRNK), intended as a bipartisan voice for human rights issues, had been established in Washington, DC; HRNK and NKFC subsequently lobbied alongside others for passage of the NKHRA.[34] In addition to opening the door to North Korean refugee resettlement inside the United

---

[33] Since 2001, the Citizens' Alliance for North Korean Human Rights.
[34] Originally titled the North Korea Freedom Act.

States, the NKHRA supported international advocacy efforts vis-à-vis North Korea itself, particularly by funding defector-led efforts to broadcast radio programs and provide other information to the people of North Korea. It also created a Special Envoy for North Korean Human Rights at the State Department – probably the most controversial piece of the NKHRA at the time, according to participants in the drafting process (author's interview 2018). The legislation had bipartisan support, including from then-Senators Brownback and Biden.

Both NKFC and HRNK have consistently involved North Korean diaspora members in their work, though the two organizations take different, largely complementary approaches. HRNK is a bipartisan, research-focused organization, which involves North Korean diaspora members as both authors of its research reports and sources of information. HRNK Director Greg Scarlatoiu described diaspora members' work with HRNK as "witnesses, report authors, and fellow advocates," helping "to elevate the legitimacy of human rights as an issue" (author's interview 2017). NKFC is a coalition rather than a single organization, and leans conservative in orientation. Compared to HRNK's think tank-like and research-focused efforts, NKFC adopts a grassroots lobbying approach to advocacy, organizing a "North Korea Freedom Week" on Capitol Hill and a global "Save North Korean Refugees" Day that in 2021 delivered appeals to stop repatriation of North Koreans to PRC diplomatic facilities in the United States and twelve other countries, in partnership with defector-focused or defector-led organizations in Japan, South Korea, and the United Kingdom. Two other organizations – the secular, nonpartisan nonprofit LINK and the Christian organization Durihana – have branches in both South Korea and the United States; both divide their time between helping defectors and refugees escape from the DPRK and providing resettlement assistance in the United States and South Korea. Thus, there is not always tight alignment between the personal political beliefs and identity of many North Korean émigrés (documented in Section 4) and the structure of the advocacy work in which they participate; although there are strong network bonds between conservative NGOs and political actors in Seoul and Washington (Reidhead in Yeo and Chubb 2018:33), these actors are embedded in a civil society network with a much broader range of orientations and approaches to political and civic engagement, including many that are bipartisan or nonpartisan.

In Japan, advocacy about and by North Korean defectors has been intertwined with the issue of abductees (Japanese citizens abducted by North Korea), which has both amplified attention and complicated advocacy efforts (Arrington in Yeo and Chubb 2018:85–108). The number of defectors from North Korea to Japan began to increase in the early 2000s; almost all were participants in the previous decades' repatriation movement (or their descendants) and became permanent residents rather than "refugees." Attention to escapees (*dappokusha*, derived from the Korean *talbukja*) increased in 2002 after the Japanese public saw video of five North Koreans, including a four-year-old girl, attempting entry to the Japanese consulate in Shenyang and being forcibly removed by Chinese police (Wan 2003). This "Shenyang incident" in May shortly preceded Kim Jong Il's admission of abductions in October, and Japanese NGOs focused on abductees subsequently began to collaborate more closely with those focused on escapees, forming a web of advocacy connections that spanned domestic resettlement, bilateral diplomacy with North Korea over the abductions, and transnational human rights advocacy.

As mentioned earlier in this section, Modu Moija and LFNKR assist North Korean escapees in Japan, but they are also members of the International Coalition to Stop Crimes Against Humanity in North Korea (ICNK), and the largest legislative and policy successes that these groups have had have not been about escapee/returnee assistance, but about broader North Korean human rights policy. The 2006 North Korean Abductions and Human Rights Act enshrined "abductions and other human rights violations" into Japanese government policy, and gave Japanese groups an avenue by which to join in global human rights advocacy efforts. Tokyo hosted forty organizations for the launch of the ICNK in 2011, and Japanese advocacy organizations pressed their government first to back the COI at the UN itself (Japan drafted the resolution creating the UNCOI), and then to host two days of COI hearings.

Escapee and abductee activists have presented their concerns to domestic Japanese courts as well, a fact that transnational human rights forums have amplified. The first of these lawsuits was an intra-diasporic conflict: in 2008, North Korean escapee Ko Jong-mi filed suit, with support from Mamorukai, against Chosen Soren (Chongryeon) in Osaka District Court, alleging that the organization had deceived returnees and asking for 11 million yen in compensation. The case was eventually denied on statute-of-limitations grounds, but the plaintiff was subsequently invited to testify in the Commission of Inquiry hearings held in Tokyo in 2013 (HRW 2018). In August 2018, five escapees (including Ko Jong-mi) brought a lawsuit in the Tokyo District Court, this time against the North Korean government, for deceiving them into a repatriation that they say violated their rights. The lawsuit has garnered international attention (Yamaguchi 2021); rather than expecting to collect on the damages they are suing for, the plaintiffs say they hope that the lawsuit will prompt the Japanese government to negotiate on behalf of remaining repatriates and their families still in North Korea. In March 2022, the court ruled that while the plaintiffs had been deceived, they had waited too long to file suit, and denied the request for damages; at the time of writing, the plaintiffs were preparing to appeal (Gale 2022).

These "anchor communities," and the transnational relationships that had developed among them, played a key role in the UN COI – a landmark achievement in human rights advocacy for North Korea, created by a resolution of the UN Human Rights Council in 2013.[35] The COI's three jurists and nine-person staff spent a year investigating "systematic, widespread and grave violations of human rights in the DPRK." They held four hearings (in Seoul, Tokyo, Washington, and London), and drew heavily on testimony provided by exiles and refugees. In London, for example, two of the five witnesses were members of the North Korean Residents' Association, and a third, North Korean refugee Jihyun Park, worked on North Korean resettlement in the United Kingdom before joining the European Alliance for Human Rights in North Korea (EAHRNK). In total, approximately eighty witnesses and experts testified, and the Commission conducted another 240 confidential interviews with defector/refugee witnesses whose identities required protection. Émigré testimony formed the core of the 372-page final report (UNCOI 2014). Chair Michael Kirby noted that, "not only were witnesses essential to our record and the story upon which we had to base our application of international law, they were also quite contrary [in being public, democratic hearings] to the method of North Korea" (author's interview 2018). After the report's release, the credibility of the testimony presented became the focal point of debate about the legitimacy of the COI itself, as the DPRK sought to discredit key witnesses and thereby undermine the integrity of the entire Commission (Section 2).

A global advocacy movement on North Korean human rights, therefore, emerged from partnership between "anchoring" communities of North Korean émigrés and host-country advocacy organizations ("animators" in Betts and Jones's (2016) terminology) in key countries such as South Korea, the United States, the United Kingdom, and Japan. In the absence of credible testimony from members of civil society inside North Korea, it is the diaspora's testimony that has given North Korea-focused activism much of its evidentiary basis and credibility. The ability of the diaspora to stand in for local actors in the "boomerang model" – where domestic and international actors coordinate to pressure repressive actors (Keck and Sikkink 1998) – is why the participation of defectors and diaspora activists in the global advocacy movement has been so "transformational" (Yeo and Chubb 2018). As one 2015 EAHRNK report noted, "Europe's North Korean refugees have become important advocates for the freedoms of their people" (Burt 2015). In the framework outlined by Vasanthakumar (2022), North Korean diaspora members have acted as

---

[35] Citizens' Alliance began UN-focused advocacy in 2003; after the creation of the COI, Citizens' Alliance ended the rotating conferences and focused on lobbying the UN itself (Hosaniak 2018:138).

witnesses to past atrocities, as present representatives of a people to whom the state has denied voice in international fora, and as dual-identity stakeholders: simultaneously citizens and active participants in the democratic societies where they now reside, but also stakeholders in a contested vision of their homeland's future.

One additional implication of the diaspora's small size is that the personal stories and commitments of key diaspora members have shaped North Korean human rights advocacy in visible and specific ways. In the United Kingdom, Jihyun Park – a North Korean refugee activist and author, as well as Conservative Party candidate for office – has focused explicitly on women's rights, drawing on her own identity as a mother and survivor of trafficking to call attention to the experiences of a diaspora that is 70 percent female and disproportionately vulnerable to gender-based violence (Park 2023). In both South Korea and the United States, Yeonmi Park drew attention to young North Korean women as victims of trafficking and sexual violence, at a time when the #MeToo moment made those experiences especially salient in media coverage and public discourse. Subsequently, her story and her explicitly conservative political orientation have generated a wide following that includes Jordan Peterson, Joe Rogan, and Candace Owens; her second book wades heavily into hot-button cultural issues in American politics, such as critical race theory and gun control.[36]

Another UK-based activist, Kim Joo Il, is the father of a child with developmental disabilities and has chosen to focus his advocacy efforts on children's rights and disability rights (Song in Yeo and Chubb 2018:215–216). Similarly, South Korea-based defector-activist (now legislator) Ji Seong-ho, who lost his leg and several fingers in a childhood train accident, began as an activist speaking on disability issues in South Korea, the United States, and the United Kingdom; at the 2018 State of the Union address in Washington, DC, he stood in the balcony and lifted his old crutches in a moment captured by cameras. More recently, a defector group in South Korea has sought to tap into global networks of transitional justice advocates to lay groundwork for a future transitional justice movement in North Korea.[37] These and other diaspora leaders have broadened the discursive framing of North Korean human rights advocacy, and diversified the face of North Korean human rights efforts beyond the movement's origin and traditional focus on civil and political rights. This diversity, in turn, allows a

---

[36] As of late February 2022, Park's podcast with Jordan Peterson had over two million views on YouTube: www.youtube.com/watch?v=8yqa-SdJtT4.

[37] Their website is available at https://en.tjwg.org/. On international networks and transitional justice, see Zvobgo (2020).

relatively small diaspora network to maintain a broader scope of engagement with human rights issues and fora, effectively broadening its support base.

Such diversity has allowed North Korean diaspora networks to engage not only on a breadth of topics, but also using a wider range of advocacy approaches. Some organizations have adopted strategies grounded in international human rights laws and directed at global institutions, while others focus on research and documentation of various human rights-related issues, while still others pursue grassroots political lobbying of host-country governments as the primary vehicle for policy change. Chubb (in Yeo and Chubb 2018:195) refers to a principles-versus-values distinction in advocacy work: principles-oriented organizations engage largely with multilateral organizations using international legal arguments for tools like the UN COI, while values-oriented organizations emphasize domestic political lobbying in key host countries to champion legislation like the NKHRA. Together, the combination contributes to the diaspora's overall political and transnational impact.

Additionally, in several important cases, involvement in transnational advocacy has provided a stepping-stone for diaspora members to pursue a career in electoral politics inside their host countries. South Korea–based Ji Seong Ho, for example, who began as a disability rights activist, founded a domestic advocacy organization (Now Action & Unity for NK Human Rights, NAUH) that subsequently allowed him to engage in transnational advocacy efforts in the United States and the United Kingdom.[38] After gaining international political experience and interacting with parliamentarians in multiple countries, he ran for legislative office in South Korea as a 2020 candidate for a conservative party. Ji, once a victim of the North Korean regime, now serves in the South Korean National Assembly alongside a former member of the North Korean elite, diplomat-turned-defector Thae Yong Ho.[39] Similarly, Jihyun Park began her career in the United Kingdom as a grassroots activist, worked at a European organization focused on North Korean human rights (EAHRNK), and then ran for elected office in northern England. These individuals demonstrate the intertwining trajectories of domestic political incorporation and transnational activism that characterize the political engagement of the North Korean diaspora; their varied pathways, when aggregated, have allowed the diaspora to pursue multiple routes to political change over time.

The pluralism and diversity just described, however, can generate fragmentation, competition, and cleavages even within a relatively small diaspora

---

[38] Indeed, one profile described Ji as someone who "does more work on North Korean human rights abroad than in Korea" (Lim and Zulawnik 2021:191).

[39] The first North Korean defector elected to the National Assembly was Cho Myung-Chul in 2014. For an interview with him, see Lim and Zulawnik (2021: 54–59).

community. Some cleavages are generational and revolve around questions of host-country integration versus homeland orientation. In Canada, for example, some younger émigrés, who spent less time in North Korea and entered Canada at younger ages, emphasize assimilation and incorporation more than ties to their birthplace (author's interview 2021). In other places, cleavages occur between North Korean resettlers and preexisting Korean diaspora populations; North Koreans diversify a diaspora traditionally oriented toward the southern half of the peninsula, but their presence can also extraterritorially replicate the peninsula's political divide, generating local tensions (Fisher 2015; Panagiotidis 2015; Han 2017).

In still other cases, tensions between North Korean émigrés and other members of the Korean diaspora arise from divergent political or policy preferences toward their ostensibly shared homeland. Although North Korean émigrés in the United States express a range of views about North Korea (Section 4), the diaspora as a group has long been "identified with conservative anticommunist politics" (Chubb in Yeo and Chubb 2018:190) – and as Section 4 showed, its members do skew conservative in terms of party affiliation. This has led leftist voices such as Hong (2013) to criticize what they view as diasporic activists' excessive focus on civil and political rights, and to castigate North Korean human rights advocates as supportive of an imperialist, violent, regime-change agenda (compare Eberstadt and Peck 2023).[40] Korean-American activist Christine Ahn, for example, has argued that if "Korean women peacemakers" determined US policy toward North Korea, there would be a peace agreement and denuclearization (Ahn et al. 2020), but some of the strongest critics of her proposals have come from North Korean émigrés. Those émigrés who view themselves as having an identity distinct from the broader Korean diaspora retain a strong focus on civil and political rights that appears to reflect fundamental underlying beliefs about what matters in democratic citizenship (Section 4), and that does not necessarily conform to the political priorities of the most vocal progressive subgroups within the Korean-American diaspora.

These tensions have played out in recent American policy debates on North Korea. In 2021, when Representative Brad Sherman sponsored the Peace on the Korean Peninsula Act, which was supported by Women Cross DMZ and Korea Peace Now! and called for pursuit of a "binding peace agreement" and establishment of liaison offices (Ahn 2021), a coalition of North Korean defector organizations wrote to ask him to withdraw his sponsorship. In their opposition letter, North Korean émigrés invoked the credibility of their direct experience

---

[40] Yoon, the South Korean founder of Citizens' Alliance, spent decades advocating for victims of anti-communist military rule in South Korea before turning his opposition to North Korean authoritarianism and human rights abuses.

inside North Korea, and implicitly contrasted their own claim to authority with organizations like Women Cross DMZ, which is led by Korean-Americans but includes no North Korean émigré representation among its leadership or board. In opposing the proposed legislation, North Korean émigrés asserted their legitimate claim to speak for the North Korean people, and offered their narrative and policy preferences as an alternative to the recommendations of Korean-American "peace activists."

A final source of intra-diasporic disagreement can occur over tactics. European advocates for North Korean human rights have often focused on diplomatic and institutional engagement, and, as noted earlier, reflect an approach grounded more in legal principles than moral values (Chubb in Yeo and Chubb 2018:191). This typically means the pursuit of incremental change through dialogues, resolutions, and demarches, a process that often contrasts with "smaller, defector-oriented North Korean human rights victims' groups who wish for more 'action'" (Narayan in Yeo and Chubb 2018:125). Most often, the preferred action in question is direct provision of information to the people of North Korea (Baek 2016). Defector-led organizations in South Korea such as Free North Korea Radio, Fighters for a Free North Korea, North Korea Strategy Center, No Chain, Now Action Unity and Human Rights, and North Korea Intellectuals Solidarity adopt this as their primary goal, as does US-based organization Lumen. Although other organizations, such as the North Korean People's Liberation Front, adopt more militant rhetoric and have petitioned (unsuccessfully) to form specific units within the ROK military, they to date have still mostly participated in information provision activities (Mackinnon 2010). Groups that wish to pursue divergent approaches sometimes express frustration with aspects of the other approach, but over time they have tended simply to adopt a division-of-labor strategy that allows for complementarity more than open conflict.

Speculation that North Korean defector activism could take a more militant turn has not been borne out (Hudson 2019; Park 2019; Shorrock 2019; Smith and Shin 2019). This speculation peaked briefly after an incident in early 2019, in which a group called Free Joseon (previously Chollima Civil Defense) raided the DPRK embassy in Madrid and proclaimed a provisional government, though later reporting suggested that the "raid" may have been a cover for preplanned defection (S. Kim 2020). The group, including former LINK co-founder Adrian Hong, had previously received attention for claiming to have rescued Kim Jong Un's nephew, Kim Han-sol, after the highly publicized assassination of his father, Kim Jong Nam, in 2017. Free Joseon counts North Korean exiles among its membership, and told one writer that it has hundreds of members across ten countries, though its actual membership is unclear (S. Kim 2020). In the aftermath of the incident, the Spanish government issued arrest warrants for several people involved in the operation. At the time of writing, one participant in the Madrid incident had been arrested and was fighting extradition to Spain; Hong was a fugitive; and Free Joseon had not engaged in public and sustained organizational activity for several years (Boot and Terry 2021). The example of Free Joseon highlights that at present, there appears to be little potential for sustained armed diasporic resistance. Instead, diasporic activists and the advocacy organizations they associate with have centered their debates on the most effective strategies for much more limited and incremental political change (M. Kim 2021) in the context of an authoritarian North Korean polity that remains relatively isolated and impervious to outside influence, even by those who once called its territory home.

6 Conclusions, Comparative Connections, and Implications

This Element has examined the formation, political beliefs, and political behavior of North Korea's emerging diaspora, as well as how North Korea's authoritarian regime seeks to manage a diaspora that has become increasingly engaged in contention and political opposition. Section 2 traced the contours of the regime's diaspora management policies, as Pyongyang seeks to dissuade, discredit, deter, and disrupt diasporic opposition abroad. The authoritarian nature of the DPRK has shaped the diaspora, and diasporic politics also, in turn, rebound to influence Pyongyang's calculus. As North Koreans leave their places of origin, Section 3 suggested that where they go is shaped by contestation over citizenship during the asylum and refugee process, with the result that the diaspora is concentrated in South Korea but also has small communities in North America, Europe, and Japan. Section 4 probed the value that North Korean émigrés place on democratic citizenship, especially its civil dimensions. Section 5 analyzed diasporic political engagement in host countries and transnationally, showing that – by intertwining domestic and transnational political participation – North Koreans abroad have acted as witnesses to lived experiences that the authoritarian state has sought to conceal; as representatives of a people to whom that state has denied political voice both internally and internationally; and as stakeholders both in their countries of resettlement and in their vision of North Korea's future.

The political dynamics of North Korea's "defector diaspora" illuminate broader comparative themes. Historically, contested citizenship and geopolitical reality collided to shape the experiences of individuals in a divided Germany as well as in mainland China and Taiwan (Peterson 2008; Hsu 2015:136–137; Panagiotidis 2015; Madokoro 2016; Chang 2020; Morris 2022). There are parallels between South Korea's juxtaposition of legal assertiveness and practical ambivalence about North Korean escapees, on the one hand, and the reluctance, on the other, of the Kuomintang in the early 1950s to accept Chinese refugees into Taiwan. The ways in which recognition of the PRC precluded migrants in Hong Kong from being classified as refugees by the international community foreshadowed the asylum rulings that prevent North Korean resettlement around the world today (Hambro 1955; Yang 2014, 2021).

Such comparisons point to common constraints, but also highlight differences that could condition contemporary diasporic identity. South Korea characterizes assistance to North Koreans primarily as helping ethnic brethren, while Taiwan today frames assistance to Hong Kong expatriates primarily as a matter of humanitarianism and civic democratic identity (Greitens and Hur 2020). In both cases, however, assistance to pro-democracy diasporic activists has been limited by the looming geopolitical risk that could come with becoming a focal point of political opposition.

Today, diasporic opposition to authoritarianism has become a global phenomenon. In 2022, Belarussian leader Svetlana Tikhanovskaya sought to build a coalition of opposition to autocrat Alexander Lukashenko from abroad, but faced questions about her ability to do so as opposition figures who remained in-country, including her husband, were imprisoned (Hopkins 2021). Hong Kong expatriates who had escaped the city's tightening political control vowed to adopt a "diasporic model of opposition" and continue campaigning from abroad, while increasing numbers of Chinese citizens sought asylum worldwide and the FBI issued warnings about PRC authorities' use of "transnational repression" to police diasporic communities (Economist 2021; AP 2021). A Facebook group created in 2017 to connect residents of Cuba with expatriates in Miami helped trigger 2021 protests against the Cuban dictatorship (Marsh 2021). Enes Kanter, an NBA player and vocal critic-in-exile of Turkey's increasingly authoritarian government, met with Tibetan diaspora members before criticizing Chinese repression, resulting in censorship of his team's games in China (Bushnell 2021). These examples underscore the potential and perils of diasporic activism in opposition to homeland authoritarian rule: when opposition is suppressed at home, transnational opposition may be the only possibility for meaningful resistance and contention, but the tyranny of distance makes it difficult for diasporas to produce sustained and meaningful political change.

Contributions

This Element has sought to make several contributions. First, descriptively, it contributes to scholarship on migration and transnational politics in East Asia. The previous sections offer new empirical data on the emergence, political perceptions, and political behavior of the North Korean diaspora, as well as on the DPRK's efforts to control that diaspora and its attendant political risks. Theoretically, the Element argues for the utility of complementing the field's traditional focus on ethnic conceptions of diaspora by systematically incorporating the study of regime type. Both the process of diaspora formation and empirical data on North Korean émigrés' identity perceptions suggest that they form a distinctive diaspora, or at minimum a distinct subgroup embedded within the larger global Korean diasporic community. Similar to recent literature in other regional contexts, the Element views diasporas as networks that are socially constructed and politically contested (Muller-Funk 2019:5); warns of the dangers of reifying ethnicity as diasporas' sole defining feature (Liu 2021); and highlights a need to pay greater attention to how intra-diasporic fragmentation and cleavage shape both the construction of diasporic identity and the political engagement of diaspora members.

Second, theoretically, this Element seeks to rigorously and systematically consider the role of regime type in diasporic politics, and to articulate specific ways in which homeland authoritarianism shapes diaspora politics. In doing so, it also seeks to bring diaspora politics more fully into contemporary debates on comparative authoritarianism. Studies of diasporic influence on homelands, and homeland policies toward diasporas, often frame their arguments with implicitly democratic logic – for example, suggesting that diasporas influence homeland politics through civil society projects and political contributions to candidates or parties (Shain and Barth 2003: 461). Other literature is economically focused; diasporas are a source of economic strength through remittances, investment, or educational capital (H. K. Lee 2005; Ye 2014).

The emergent North Korean diaspora, however, suggests that regime type matters: the DPRK's approach to diaspora management is fundamentally shaped by the political logic of authoritarian rule, while diasporic migration choices, perceptions of politics, and patterns of engagement in political action are all shaped by the nondemocratic nature of the North Korean homeland. This is not to suggest that we should entirely eschew traditional lenses on diasporic politics, but to urge scholars to think more systematically about how regime type shapes intra-diasporic identity, political perceptions, and networked diasporic opposition. It also calls on scholars of comparative authoritarianism to more systematically treat diaspora management as a regular component of the toolkit of autocratic political survival.

Third, evidence from North Korea offers a cautionary scoping tale for those who emphasize the potential for diasporic mobilization to challenge authoritarian rule (Betts and Jones 2016). Much current scholarship on diasporic roles in contention and opposition to authoritarianism focuses on the Arab Spring, where the diaspora successfully mobilized contention; however, this mobilization generally relied on the availability of Western social media tools to bridge the distance between diasporic activists and those on the ground in the homeland (Muller-Funk 2019; Moss 2020, 2021; Esberg and Siegel 2022; Nugent and Siegel 2023). These tools are, at best, unevenly available across autocracies. In some cases, like North Korea, they are almost completely prohibited, while in others, domestic rather than Western platforms have higher market share, and platforms are subject to regulation, surveillance, and use by increasingly sophisticated dictatorships – a phenomenon that's led to a growing literature on "digital" or "techno-authoritarianism." It is simply an empirical unknown, for example, whether the PRC platform WeChat – widely used by the Chinese diaspora to communicate with family in China – would facilitate cross-border mobilization in the same ways that Twitter did in the Arab Spring, given China's regulation of the tech sector and a National Intelligence Law that requires companies to provide information to party-state actors. Scholars and policymakers should therefore be cautious in their estimations of diasporic potential for effective anti-regime mobilization until further research has probed the scope conditions under which such mobilization is (1) possible to catalyze, and (2) likely to be successful after catalyzation.

Implications for Theory and Policy

This Element's findings have important implications for future research. Its core argument is that regime type matters for diasporic politics and political engagement – but autocracy itself is a heterogeneous category. Future research could examine how variations among autocracies shape and condition the opportunity structure for diasporic contention and activism, as well as when these efforts are more or less likely to affect different outcomes in the homeland (whether the outcome of interest is regime change or something less transformative). As noted earlier, current literature on diasporic contention is influenced strongly by the Arab Spring, but outcomes even within the Arab Spring were heterogeneous (Moss 2020), and the most successful cases often relied on tools not available to all activists, as well as on opportunity structures that do not exist in many authoritarian regimes. Juxtaposing these cases with North Korea suggests that comparativists must carefully consider the scope conditions of their arguments, and that further comparative research is necessary – to adequately account for variations in the success and failure of diasporic mobilization and political action, and to identify clearly what patterns of diasporic political activity stabilize or undermine homeland authoritarian rule, under which combinations of domestic and international conditions.

Second, regimes change over time – but the interaction between regime change and diasporic political engagement is also poorly understood. Placed in historical and comparative context, this is a significant oversight. Diaspora communities in post-socialist Europe, even those that had been isolated from their homelands for long periods, played significant and varied roles in both democratization processes and post-democratization political life (Koinova 2009). Iraqi elites-in-exile significantly impacted the 2003 invasion-turned-regime-change in Iraq, though initial high levels of political engagement have waned as returning émigrés grew disappointed in continued corruption and sectarian exclusion in Iraqi politics (Kadhum 2021). The combined effects of attempted and failed regime transformations in China and Eastern Europe in 1989 created a Chinese diaspora in Central and Eastern Europe where none existed before – especially Hungary, whose resistance to Soviet domination held particular fascination for Chinese emigrants (Liu 2021:40–43). The Korean diaspora itself was deeply involved in homeland struggles for anti-colonial liberation (Kim 2011; Park 2015), and afterward South Korea's diaspora centered on a homeland that moved from military-authoritarian rule to a thriving, cosmopolitan democracy. Future scholarship could systematize and extend existing knowledge of how diasporic actors affect regime change, and could also begin to examine the largely-unaddressed question of how regime transition shapes the diaspora and/or alters its patterns of political engagement.

Third, increased emphasis on authoritarian-oriented waves of emigration and diaspora formation highlights the value of understanding how newer, oppositional or "defector" diasporas relate to previously existing migrant communities. When refugees escaping homeland authoritarianism join already established co-ethnic communities, how do those existing communities shape and condition patterns of political incorporation and subsequent political behavior, and vice versa? How do migrants that engage in diasporic opposition relate to politically inactive or pro-regime subgroups, whether these subgroups come from previous migratory waves or the same one? Under what conditions do resulting intra-diasporic cleavages shape political incorporation, perceptions of citizenship, and political behavior? Future research could fruitfully investigate all of these questions.

Finally, this Element has implications for policy. For policymakers and activists, the primary lesson is probably a cautionary one: the experience of Arab diasporas during the 2011 uprisings should not be taken as a universally applicable precedent. Not all authoritarian regimes offer their diasporas the kind of opportunity structures and connective networks that made the transnational activism of the Arab Spring possible. Moreover, the degree and type of diasporic political incorporation into one or more host countries is likely to shape a diaspora's subsequent capability and willingness to advocate for political change, whether that advocacy occurs by influencing the foreign policies of host countries toward the homeland, or by directly supporting activists on the ground in the homeland itself. Policymakers should recognize that in many cases of authoritarian rule, diasporic opposition and advocacy offer one of the only spaces where meaningful voice and contention are possible and significant, while maintaining realistic expectations about the nature and scope of diasporic impact.

These findings also have important implications for the potential unification of the Korean peninsula. As Sections 4 and 5 highlighted, émigrés in third countries have played critical roles as witnesses and spokespeople in transnational advocacy against North Korea's human rights abuses, and will almost certainly continue to do so. The émigré community based in South Korea, however, is likely to carry more "stakeholder" weight in discussions about unification, given its geographic proximity to North Korea; critical mass in terms of population size; diasporic sentiment and support for unification expressed by North Korean resettlers in the South; and the role that the South Korean government accords to North Korea–born individuals in its current vision of the unification process. Indeed, the proposition that integration of North Koreans in South Korea is a "test case" for unification, and the expectation that North Korean defectors will play a leading role in any future unification process, are both commonplace in Seoul, one reason why dissatisfaction among North Korean defectors in the South is widely perceived as policy failure on the part of the ROK government (author's interviews, 2014, 2016; see also Go 2014; Kim et al. 2017:46; Bae 2018; Suh n.d.). As yet, there has been little systematic discussion in the ROK of the role that a *global* diaspora could or should play in unification – a topic worth systematically considering.

Despite evidence on the importance thus far of diasporic "anchors" for successful transnational advocacy efforts, recommendations to diversify support for the North Korean diaspora across the international community[41] have born relatively little fruit. This may be due to the environment created by tighter migration controls in North Korea, US freezes on immigration during the Trump administration, and the generally limiting effects of the COVID-19 pandemic, so it is not clear whether that trend is a temporary one. It is therefore an open question how the current global distribution of North Korean diaspora communities will change in the future, as well as how the evolution of these communities might affect attitudes toward and engagement in unification scenarios, by host-country governments and diasporic communities themselves.

---

[41] For example, by strengthening resettlement and support programs in the United States (Cha and Walsh 2016).

What is certain is that the North Korean diaspora, though small in number, has learned enough about democratic citizenship to engage actively in it, and in doing so, members of the diaspora have had a visible effect on host-country and international policy toward their homeland. While the prospects for diasporic activism achieving wholesale democratization or regime change seem small at present, the rise of criticism from within the diaspora is a development taken seriously as a threat by the regime in Pyongyang. In the years to come, the political dynamics and global impact of the North Korean diaspora will continue to be shaped by host and homeland government policies; the diaspora's size and dispersion; the extent and specific form of émigrés' political identities and incorporation in host countries; and the distribution and diversity of diasporic voices. As this trajectory unfolds, North Korean émigrés will continue to add their voices to the global Korean community, contributing to its evolving diaspora and writing a history of North Korea that extends not only past the peninsula itself, but beyond the reach of the homeland authoritarian regime.

Appendix: Survey of North Koreans in the United States

Politics of the North Korean Diaspora draws on an original, bilingual survey conducted in Fall 2021 among North Korean migrants and refugees in the United States. Survey enumeration procedures and language were approved by the University of Texas-Austin's Institutional Review Board in July 2021 (STUDY00001394). The survey design was informed by ~16 years of discussion/interaction with and interviews of resettled North Koreans in the United States and South Korea, as well as interviews, participant observation, and conversations with organizations that focus on North Korea-related advocacy and resettlement assistance in South Korea, the United States, and the United Kingdom. Both English and Korean versions of the survey were pre-reviewed by a member of the North Korean community in the U.S. to ensure that the survey question framing and language choices made sense to respondents within the community.

Participants were recruited via snowball sampling, beginning with the Principal Investigator's contacts. To offset the limitations of this method, encourage breadth of representation from the North Korean community, and minimize the potential for bias introduced by researcher positionality and personal network limitations, the survey had multiple "seeds," or starting points: the PI partnered with six service and advocacy organizations that work with North Koreans in the U.S., each with its own network. These organizations circulated a survey link to their North Koreans contacts and received a small donation as compensation for staff time and assistance. The survey itself was administered online via Qualtrics in both English and Korean. In addition to questions developed by the PI, it contained questions asked in global surveys as well as questions asked in previous surveys of North Korean defectors/refugees in South Korea. Questions were a mix of multiple-choice and open-ended questions; the latter allowed respondents to provide qualitative detail if they chose.

52 respondents completed the survey. Participants could choose to skip particular questions, so across survey items, the number of respondents ranged from 45 to 52. Respondents could opt in to receive a $100 gift card in compensation for their time at the end; 40 of 52 chose to do so. Participants were 68% female, 32% male, making the gender composition of the sample similar to the known composition of the North Korean resettler population in South Korea (~70% female). They included some of the ~230 individuals who entered the

United States as refugees under the 2004 North Korean Human Rights Act, as well as some individuals who previously lived in South Korea and had subsequently moved to the U.S. to study or work. All were adults, ranging in age from 21 to 78; the mean age was 39. Respondents reported departing North Korea between 1997 and 2018, and arriving in the U.S. between 2007 and 2021; the mean length of residence in the U.S. was between 7–8 years. The majority had transited at least two countries between North Korea and the U.S. (usually China and either Thailand or South Korea) and had lived in anywhere from 1 to 6 U.S. states since their arrival.

References

Abdelaaty, Lamis Elmy. 2021. *Discrimination and Delegation: Explaining State Responses to Refugees*. Oxford University Press.

Adamson, Fiona. 2020. "Non-state Authoritarianism and Diaspora Politics." *Global Networks* 20/1:150–169.

AFP. 1997. "N. Korean Defector Declared Dead after Attack." *Agence France-Presse*, 25 February.

Ahn, Christine. 2021. "How Congress Can Advance Peace with North Korea." *The Hill*, 12 July. https://thehill.com/opinion/international/562634-how-congress-can-advance-peace-with-north-korea.

Ahn, Christine, Yifat Susskind, and Cindy Weisneir. 2020. "Women of Color Should Be the Ones Remaking American Foreign Policy." *Newsweek*, 17 November. www.newsweek.com/women-color-should-ones-remaking-us-foreign-policy-opinion-1548013.

Al Jazeera. 2010. "S Korea Arrests 'N Korean Agent'." 20 October. https://www.aljazeera.com/news/2010/10/20/s-korea-arrests-n-korean-agent.

Al Jazeera. 2018. "Canada Deports North Korean Asylum Seekers." 18 February. www.aljazeera.com/news/2018/02/canada-deports-north-korean-asylum-seekers-180218144353430.html.

Aleman, Jose, and Dwayne Woods. 2014. "No Way Out: Travel Restrictions and Authoritarian Regimes." *Migration and Development* 3/2:285–305.

Anna, Cara. 2015. "North Korea to UN: Human Rights Resolution Is Illegal." *Associated Press*, 4 February. www.sandiegouniontribune.com/sdut-north-korea-to-un-human-rights-resolution-is-2015feb04-story.html.

Arteburn, Jason. 2018. *Dispatched: Mapping Overseas Forced Labor in North Korea's Proliferation Finance System*. C4ADS. https://c4ads.org/reports/dispatched/.

Associated Press. 1997. "Attack on Defector Escalates North–South Enmity in Korea." 16 February.

Associated Press. 2015. "A Look at Past Car Accidents Involving N. Korean Officials." 30 December. www.dailyherald.com/article/20151230/news/312309944.

Associated Press. 2021. "Hong Kong Activists Say Fight for Democracy to Continue Abroad." 15 March. https://apnews.com/article/asia-pacific-hong-kong-elections-democracy-beijing-1be5434b9c2c215600f12d3bf3bad343.

Bae, S. J. 2018. "Difficulties Integrating North Korean Defectors Suggest Challenges in Reunifying Korea." RAND, 11 June. www.rand.org/blog/ 2018/06/difficulties-integrating-north-korean-defectors-suggest.html.

Baek, Jieun. 2016. *North Korea's Hidden Revolution: How the Information Underground Is Transforming a Closed Society.* Yale University Press.

BBC. 1991. "Burmese Court Rules against North Korea on 1983 Bombing." 19 February.

BBC. 2016. "North Korean Official's Death Raises Questions." 5 January.

BBC. 2017. "Kim Jong Nam: Interpol 'Red Notice' for N. Koreans." 16 March. www.bbc.com/news/world-asia-39288864.

BBC. 2019. "North Korean Fishermen 'Killed 16 Colleagues' Before Fleeing to South." 7 November. www.bbc.com/news/world-asia-50329588.

Bell, Markus. 2013. "Manufacturing Kinship in a Nation Divided: An Ethnographic Study of North Korean Refugees in South Korea." *Asia Pacific Journal of Anthropology* 14/3:240–255.

Bell, Markus. 2016. "Making and Breaking Family: North Korea's Zainichi Returnees and 'the Gift'." *Asian Anthropology* 15/3:260–276.

Bell, Markus. 2019. "Reimagining North Korea: The Korean Diaspora's Changing Relationship to the Homeland." *Asia Pacific Journal of Anthropology* 20/1:22–41.

Bell, Markus. 2021. *Outsiders: Memories of Migration to and From North Korea.* Berghahn Books.

Bell, Markus, and Jay Song. 2018. "North Korean Secondary Asylum in the UK." *Migration Studies* 6/1:1–20.

Berlinger, Joshua. 2019. "As Last Jailed Kim Jong Nam Killing Suspect Freed, a Gripping Murder Mystery Ends with a Whimper." CNN, 3 May. www.cnn .com/2019/05/02/asia/kim-jong-nam-trial-intl/index.html.

Bermeo, Nancy. 2007. "War and Democratization: Lessons from the Portuguese Experience." *Democratization* 14/3:388–406.

Betts, Alexander, and Will Jones. 2016. *Mobilising the Diaspora: How Refugees Challenge Authoritarianism.* Cambridge University Press.

Boot, Max, and Sue Mi Terry. 2021. "Ex-Marine Tried to Help North Koreans Defect. Now He Faces Decades in Prison." *Washington Post*, 2 May. www .washingtonpost.com/opinions/2021/05/02/christopher-ahn-north-korea-dip lomat-defect-prison/.

Brubaker, Rogers, and Kim Jaaeun. 2011. "Transborder Membership Politics in Germany and Korea." *European Journal of Sociology* 52/1:21–75.

Brubaker, Rogers. 2005. "The Diaspora Diaspora." *Ethnic and Racial Studies* 28/1:1–19.

Burt, James. 2015. "A Case for Clarification: European Asylum Policy and North Korean Refugees." European Alliance for Human Rights in North Korea, March.

Bush Center. 2019. "President Bush Meets with North Korean Refugees." 21 June. www.bushcenter.org/about-the-center/newsroom/press-releases/2019/06/president-bush-meets-with-north-korean-refugees.html.

Bush Institute. 2014. *U.S.-Based North Korean Refugees: A Qualitative Study.* https://gwbcenter.imgix.net/Resources/gwb_north_korea_executive_summary_r4.pdf.

Bushnell, Henry. 2021. "Why Enes Kanter Spoke Out Against China." Yahoo! Sports, 21 October. https://sports.yahoo.com/why-enes-kanter-spoke-out-against-china-011555552.html.

Camp, Roderic Ai. 2003. "Learning Democracy in Mexico and the United States." *Mexican Studies/Estudios Mexicanos* 19/1:3–27.

Campbell, Emma. 2016. *South Korea's New Nationalism: The End of "One Korea"?* Lynne Rienner.

Carter, Erin, and Brett Carter. 2022. "When Autocrats Threaten Citizens with Violence: Evidence from China." *British Journal of Political Science* 52/2:671–696.

Castles, Stephen. 1995. "How Nation-States Respond to Immigration and Ethnic Diversity." *New Community* 21/3:298–308.

Cathcart, Adam. 2019. "North Korean Citizens in Changbai." SinoNK, 21 January. https://sinonk.com/2019/01/21/north-korean-citizens-in-changbai-social-insurance-residency-rights-and-chinese-informants/.

Cathcart, Adam, Christopher Green, and Steven Denney. 2014. "How Authoritarian Regimes Maintain Domain Consensus: North Korea's Information Strategies in the Kim Jong-un Era." *Review of Korean Studies* 17/2(December):145–178.

Cha, Victor, and Christopher Walsh. 2016. "Refugees Might Be the New Administration's Best Friends on North Korea Strategy." *Foreign Policy*, 12 December. https://foreignpolicy.com/2016/12/12/refugees-might-be-the-new-administrations-best-friends-on-north-korea-strategy.

Chang, David Cheng. 2020. *The Hijacked War.* Stanford University Press.

Chang, Kyung-sup. 2012. "Developmental Citizenship in Perspective: The South Korean Case and Beyond." In *Contested Citizenship in East Asia: Developmental Policies, National Unity, and Globalization* (Kyung-sup Chang and Bryan Turner, eds.; Routledge), pp. 182–202.

Chauvet, Lisa, and Marion Mercier. 2014. "Do Return Migrants Transfer Political Norms to Their Origin Country? Evidence from Mali." *Journal of Comparative Economics* 42/3:630–651.

Chavez, Nicole. 2021. "North Koreans and Their Families in the US Have Waited 70 Years for a Reunion. Time Is Running Out." CNN, 25 July. www.cbs58.com/news/korean-americans-separated-by-war-have-waited-70-years-for-a-reunion-their-time-is-running-out.

Cho, Dong-Wun, and Yong-Tae Kim. 2011. "Study on Settlement Services for North Korean Defectors." *Journal of Korean Public Police and Security Services* 8/2:25–50.

Choe, Sang-hun. 2020. "South Korea Confirms a Defector Swam Back to the North." *New York Times*, 27 July. www.nytimes.com/2020/07/27/world/asia/north-korea-defector-coronavirus.html.

Choi Ha-young. 2016. "Korean-Chinese Pastor-Activist Killed on North Korean Border." *NK News*, 2 May. www.nknews.org/2016/05/korean-chinese-pastor-activist-killed-on-north-korean-border/.

Choo, Hae Yeon. 2006. "Gendered Modernity and Ethnicized Citizenship: North Korean Settlers in Contemporary South Korea." *Gender and Society* 20/5:576–604.

Choo, Hae Yeon. 2016. *Decentering Citizenship: Gender, Labor, and Migrant Rights in South Korea.* Stanford University Press.

Choson Sinbo. 2015. "재일조선인에 대한 헤이트스피치는 인권침해, 일본정부가 첫 권고 [Hate Speech against Korean Residents in Japan is a Violation of Human Rights – Recommendation of Japanese Government]." 24 December. http://chosonsinbo.com/2015/12/20151224suk/.

Choson Sinbo. 2018. "[Chongryon Participates in UN Minority Forum for First Time, Reports Discrimination against Choson Schools & Korean Youth in Japan]." 29 March.

Choson Sinbo. 2019. "부당한 차별적조치의 철회를/조선유치반의 제외를 노리는 일본당국 [Withdraw Unjust Discriminatory Measures – Japanese Authorities' Exclusion of Chosun Kindergarteners]." 2 September. www.chosonsinbo.com/2019/09/hj190902/.

Chosun Ilbo. 2006. "U.S. State Department Talks Defectors with Seoul." 26 May. http://english.chosun.com/site/data/html_dir/2006/05/26/2006052661022.html?related_all.

Chosun Ilbo. 2011. "N. Korean Defectors Flock to UK." 15 July. http://english.chosun.com/site/data/html_dir/2011/07/15/2011071500450.html.

Chubb, Danielle. *Contentious Activism and Inter-Korean Relations.* Columbia University Press. 2014.

Chung, Byung Ho. 2008. "Between Defector and Migrant: Identities and Strategies of North Koreans in South Korea." *Korean Studies* 32:1–27.

Chung, Erin. 2006. *Immigration and Citizenship in Japan.* Cambridge University Press.

CNN. 2016. "North Korean Families Plead for Defectors to Return." 11 May. www.cnn.com/videos/world/2016/05/11/north-korea-defector-families-pkg-ripley.cnn.

Cohen, Robin. 1997. *Global Diasporas: An Introduction*. University of Washington Press.

Coppedge, Michael, et al. 2011. "Conceptualizing and Measuring Democracy: A New Approach." *Perspectives on Politics* 9/2:247–267.

De Wind, J., et al. 2012. "Korean Development and Migration." *Journal of Ethnic and Migration Studies* 38/3:371–388.

Delano, Alexandra, and Alan Gamlen. 2014. "Comparing and Theorizing State–Diaspora Relations." *Political Geography* 41:43–53.

Demick, Barbara. 2006. "She's Fled Both Koreas, and Controversy Has Followed." *Los Angeles Times*, 8 May. http://articles.latimes.com/2006/may/08/world/fg-asylum8.

Demick, Barbara. 2011a. "North Korea Suspected in Poison-Needle Attacks." *Los Angeles Times*, 9 October. www.latimes.com/world/la-xpm-2011-oct-09-la-fg-north-korea-poison-20111010-story.html.

Demick, Barbara. 2011b. "Poison Needle Attacks Target Activists; North Korea Suspected to Be Retaliating against Anti-Kim Jong Il Messages from South." *Los Angeles Times*, 12 October.

Denney, Steven, and Christopher Green. 2018. "Unification in Action? The National Identity of North Korean Defector-Migrants: Insights and Implications." *Korean Economic Institute of America: Academic Paper Series*, 1 October. https://keia.org/publication/unification-in-action-the-national-identity-of-north-korean-defector-migrants-insights-and-implications/.

Denney, Steven, Christopher Green, and Peter Ward. 2019. *Old Values, New Orders: Where Do North Koreans Fit in the New South Korea?* Leiden Asia Center. PDF available online at https://sinonk.com/2019/05/14/new-values-and-old-orders-where-do-north-koreans-fit-in-the-new-south-korea/.

Desilver, Drew. 2021. "Turnout Soared In 2020 . . ." Pew Research, 28 January. www.pewresearch.org/fact-tank/2021/01/28/turnout-soared-in-2020-as-nearly-two-thirds-of-eligible-u-s-voters-cast-ballots-for-president/.

Dong-A Ilbo. 2013. "Assassination Attempts Disguised in Car Accidents in N. Korea." 10 May.

Dong-A Ilbo. 2020. "국정원 "10년간 재입북자 29명 . . . 협박, 국내범죄 등 사유." 22 September. www.donga.com/news/Politics/article/all/20200922/103048687/1.

Draudt, Darcie. 2019. "Multiculturalism as State Development Policy in Global Korea." In *Korea and the World* (Gregg Brazinsky, ed.; Rowman & Littlefield), pp. 157–178.

Dukalskis, Alex. 2021. *Making the World Safe for Dictatorship.* Oxford University Press.

East–West Center and the National Committee on North Korea. 2019. "North Korea in the World." www.northkoreaintheworld.org/diplomatic/dprk-embassies-worldwide.

Eberstadt, Nicholas. 2007. *The North Korean Economy.* Transaction Publishers.

Eberstadt, Nicholas, and Lawrence Peck. 2023. "Discussing the Pro-North Korea Movement in the USA." American Enterprise Institute (multimedia presentation). 29 September. www.aei.org/multimedia/discussing-the-pro-north-korean-movement-in-the-usa-presentation-by-eberstadt-and-peck/.

Economist. 2021. "Under Xi the Number of Chinese Asylum Seekers Has Shot Up." 28 July. www.economist.com/graphic-detail/2021/07/28/under-xi-jinping-the-number-of-chinese-asylum-seekers-has-shot-up?utm.

Esberg, Jane, and Alexandra Siegel. 2022. "How Exile Shapes Online Opposition: Evidence from Venezuela." *American Political Science Review*, 1–18.

Fahy, Sandra. 2019. *Dying for Rights: Putting North Korea's Human Rights Abuses on the Record.* Columbia University Press.

Feith, David. 2013. "Park Sang Hak: North Korea's 'Enemy Zero'." *Wall Street Journal*, 5 July. www.wsj.com/articles/SB10001424127887324853704578585961242121902?mod=hp_opinion.

Fifield, Anna. 2019. *The Great Successor. The Divinely Perfect Destiny of Brilliant Comrade Kim Jong Un.* PublicAffairs.

Fischer, Paul. 2015. "The Korean Republic of New Malden." *The Independent*, 22 February. www.independent.co.uk/news/uk/home-news/the-korean-republic-of-new-malden-how-surrey-became-home-to-the-70-year-old-conflict-10063055.html.

Furey, Anthony. 2019. "Don't Deport Us: North Korean Defectors Plead Their Case." *Toronto Sun*, 3 September. https://torontosun.com/news/national/dont-deport-us-north-korean-defectors-plead-their-case.

Gale, Alastair. 2022. "North Korean Lured Japanese by Promising Paradise. Some Escapees are Now Suing Kim Jong Un – 'We Were Deceived'." *Wall Street Journal*, 21 October. www.wsj.com/articles/north-korea-lured-japanese-by-promising-paradise-some-escapees-are-now-suing-kim-jong-un-we-were-deceived-11666360802.

Gallagher, Mary. 2020. "Corporatist Organization in a Pluralist Setting." Working Paper.

Gamlen, Alan, Michael E. Cummings, and Paul M. Vaaler. 2017. "Explaining the Rise of Diaspora Institutions." *Journal of Ethnic and Migration Studies* 45/4:492–516.

Gauthier, Brandon. 2014. "The American–Korean Friendship and Information Center and North Korean Public Diplomacy, 1971–1976." *Yonsei Journal of International Studies* 6/1: 151–162.

Gerson, Daniela. 2006. "How Ms. Ma of North Korea Seeks Asylum in America." *New York Sun*, 15 March. www.nysun.com/new-york/how-ms-ma-of-north-korea-seeks-asylum-in-america/29143/.

Glasius, Marlies. 2018. "Extraterritorial Authoritarian Practices: A Framework." *Globalizations* 15/2:179–197.

Gleason, Brian. 2012. "Double Defectors: Signifiers of North Korea's Strategic Shift." *SinoNK*, 6 December. https://sinonk.com/2012/12/06/double-defect ors-signifiers-of-pyongyangs-strategic-shift/.

Go, Myong Hyun. 2014. "Resettling in South Korea: Challenges for Young North Korean Refugees." Asan Institute for Policy Studies. http://en.asaninst .org/contents/resettling-in-south-korea-challenges-foryoung-north-korean-refugees.

Goldring, Edward. 2021. *Purges: A Dictator's Fight to Survive*. Book manuscript.

Goodman, Sarah Wallace. 2022. *Citizenship in Hard Times: How Ordinary People Respond to Democratic Threat*. Cambridge University Press.

Government of Canada. 2015. X (Re), 2015 CanLII 105649 (CA IRB). www .canlii.org/en/ca/irb/doc/2015/2015canlii105649/2015canlii105649.html? searchUrlHash=AAAAAQALbm9ydGgga29yZWEAAAAAAQ&resultInd ex=4.

Government of Canada, Immigration and Refugee Board [IRB]. 2016a. "Jurisprudential Guides – Decision TB4-05778." 27 June. www .canlii.org/en/ca/irb/doc/2016/2016canlii73070/2016canlii73070.html? searchUrlHash=AAAAAQALbm9ydGgga29yZWEAAAAAAQ&resultInd ex=2.

Government of Canada, Immigrant and Refugee Board [IRB]. 2016b. *Decision TB4-05778*. Refugee Appeals Division. Toronto, Ontario, 27 June. www .refworld.org/cases,IRBC,5a26e1d04.html.

Government of Canada, Kim v. Canada. 2010. [*Kim, Min Jung* v. *M.C.I.* (F.C., no. IMM-5625-09)], 30 June, 2010 FC 720. www.refworld.org/pdfid/ 5476e8334.pdf.

Government of the Netherlands, Council of State. 2014. Pronunciation 201404877/1/V2. www.raadvanstate.nl/uitspraken/zoeken-in-uitspraken/ tekst-uitspraak.html?id=80141.

Government of the Republic of Korea. 1987. *Constitution of the Republic of Korea*. http://korea.assembly.go.kr/res/low_01_read.jsp?boardid= 1000000035.

Government of the Republic of Korea. 2010. *Nationality Act*. http://elaw.klri.re
.kr/eng_service/lawView.do?hseq=18840&lang=ENG.

Government of the Republic of Korea. 2019. *North Korean Refugees Protection
and Settlement Support Act*. http://elaw.klri.re.kr/eng_service/lawView.do?
hseq=32024&lang=ENG.

Government of the Republic of Korea, Ministry of Foreign Affairs [MOFA].
2013. *Regulation on the Establishment and Operation of the National
Community Overseas Team*.

Government of the Republic of Korea, Ministry of Unification [MOU]. 2013,
2015. *Pukhan it'al chumin chŏngch'ak chiwŏn silmu p'yŏllam* [Settlement
Support Handbook for North Korean Refugees]. Seoul: Ministry of
Unification [T'ongilbu].

Government of the Republic of Korea, Ministry of Unification [MOU]. 2023.
"Policy on North Korean Defectors." www.unikorea.go.kr/eng_unikorea/
relations/statistics/defectors.

Government of the United Kingdom. 2011. *KK and Others* (Nationality: North
Korea) Korea CG [2011] UKUT 00092. https://tribunalsdecisions.service
.gov.uk/utiac/37601.

Government of the United Kingdom. 2014. *GP and Others* (South Korean
citizenship) Korea CG [2014] UKUT 391. https://tribunalsdecisions.ser
vice.gov.uk/utiac/2014-ukut-391.

Government of the United Kingdom. 2015. *AA/09869/2014 & AA/09870/2014*
[August]. https://tribunalsdecisions.service.gov.uk/utiac/aa-09869-2014-aa-
09870-2014.

Government of the United Kingdom, Home Office. 2014. "Country Information
and Guidance Democratic People's Republic of Korea (North Korea):
Opposition to the Regime." www.gov.uk/government/uploads/system/
uploads/attachment_data/file/380630/CIG_DRK_opposition_to_the_
Regime_v_1_0.pdf.

Government of the United Kingdom, Home Office. 2016. "Country Information
and Guidance: North Korea: Opposition to the Regime." October. www.gov
.uk/government/publications/north-korea-country-policy-and-information-
notes.

Government of the United Kingdom, Office for National Statistics [ONS].
2017. *Population by Country of Birth and Nationality*. London.

Government of the United States. 2004. *North Korean Human Rights Act*. www
.gpo.gov/fdsys/pkg/PLAW-108publ333/content-detail.html.

Government of the United States, Board of Immigration Appeals [BIA]. 2007.
24 I&N Dec. 133. www.justice.gov/sites/default/files/eoir/legacy/2014/07/
25/3560.pdf.

Government of the United States, Government Accounting Office [GAO]. 2010. "Humanitarian Assistance: Status of North Korean Refugee Resettlement and Asylum in the United States." 24 June. www.gao.gov/products/gao-10-691.

Government of the United States, Department of the Treasury. 2020. "Treasury Sanctions Entities Involved in Exporting Workers from North Korea." 19 November. https://home.treasury.gov/news/press-releases/sm1189.

Green, Christopher, and Steven Denney. 2021. "North Korean Patriotism: Assessing the Successes and Failures of a Nation." *Korea Journal* 61/1:154–185.

Green, Christopher, Steven Denney, and Brian Gleason. 2015. "The Whisper in the Ear: Re-Defector Press Conferences as an Information Management Tool." *KEI Academic Paper Series* (March).

Greitens, Sheena Chestnut. 2016. *Dictators and Their Secret Police: Coercive Institutions and State Violence.* Cambridge University Press.

Greitens, Sheena Chestnut. 2019. "Explaining Economic Order in North Korea." In *Korea and the World: New Frontiers in Korean Studies* (Gregg Brazinsky, ed.; Rowman & Littlefield), pp. 129–158.

Greitens, Sheena Chestnut. 2021. "The Geopolitics of Citizenship: Evidence from North Korean Claims to Membership in the South." *Journal of Korean Studies* 26/1: 117–151.

Greitens, Sheena Chestnut, and Aram Hur. 2020. "Why Taiwan's Assistance to Hong Kong Matters." *Foreign Policy*, 2 July. https://foreignpolicy.com/2020/07/02/why-taiwans-assistance-to-hong-kong-matters/.

Greitens, Sheena Chestnut, and Myunghee Lee. 2023. "How Do Refugees Choose Migration Routes? Evidence from North Korea." Working paper.

Greitens, Sheena Chestnut, and Benjamin Katzeff Silberstein. 2021. "Toward Market Leninism in North Korea: Assessing Kim Jong Un's First Decade." *Asian Survey* 62/2:211–239.

Greitens, Sheena Chestnut, Lee Morgenbesser, and Tore Wig. 2023. "Autocratic Assassins." Working paper, September.

Griffiths, James, and K. J. Kwon. 2017. "Celebrity Defector Returns to North Korea, Stars in Propaganda Video." CNN, 18 July. www.cnn.com/2017/07/18/asia/north-korea-defector-propaganda/index.html.

Grzelczyk, Virginie. 2014. "New Approaches to North Korean Politics after Reunification." *Communist and Post-Communist Studies* 47:170–190.

Guarnizo, Luis Eduardo, Alejandro Portes, and William Haller. 2003. "Assimilation and Transnationalism: Determinants of Transnational Political Action among Contemporary Migrants." *American Journal of Sociology* 108/6):1211–1248.

Haas, Benjamin. 2018. "Forever Strangers': The North Korean Defectors Who Want to Go Back." *Guardian*, 26 April. www.theguardian.com/world/2018/apr/26/forever-strangers-the-north-korean-defectors-who-want-to-go-back.

Haggard, Stephan. 2015. "The Case Against – and For – Shin Dong-Hyuk." *Witness to Transformation* (blog), 22 January. www.piie.com/blogs/north-korea-witness-transformation/case-against-and-shin-dong-hyuk.

Haggard, Stephen, and Marcus Noland. 2011. *Witness to Transformation: Refugee Insights into North Korea*. Peterson Institute.

Halloran, Richard. 1974. "Seoul Says North Ordered Park Slain." *New York Times*, 18 August. www.nytimes.com/1974/08/18/archives/seoul-says-north-ordered-park-slain-confession-alleged-political.html.

Hambro, Edvard. 1955. *The Problem of Chinese Refugees in Hong Kong: Report Submitted to the United Nations High Commissioner for Refugees*. A.W. Sitfhoff.

Hamlin, Rebecca. 2021. *Crossing: How We Label and React to People on the Move*. Stanford University Press.

Han, Enze. 2017. "Bifurcated Homeland and Diaspora Politics in China and Taiwan toward the Overseas Chinese in Southeast Asia." *Journal of Ethnic and Migration Studies* 45/4:577–594.

Han, Ju Hui Judy. 2013. "Beyond Safe Haven: A Critique of Christian Custody of North Korean Migrants in China." *Critical Asian Studies* 45/4:533–560.

Hana Foundation (Republic of Korea). 2021. *Bukhan Italjumin Siltaejosa* [A Survey of North Korean Defectors]. Seoul.

Hankyoreh. 2006a. "North Korean Defectors Seeking Asylum at US Embassies." 8 May. www.hani.co.kr/arti/english_edition/e_international/121585.html.

Hankyoreh. 2006b. "Seoul Asks for Explanation for Court-Approved Asylum for N. Korean Defectors." 17 August. www.hani.co.kr/arti/english_edition/e_international/150004.html.

HanVoice. 2016. "Submission to the Standing Senate Committee on Human Rights." 13 April.

HanVoice. 2021. "HanVoice Announces Historic Program." 26 October. https://hanvoice.ca/blog/pressrelease.

Harden, Blaine. 2015. "Escape from Camp 14: Revised Foreword." https://blaineharden.com/escape-from-camp-14-reviews/.

Harlan, Chico. 2012. "North Korean Defector Manipulated into Returning, Claim Friends in Seoul." *Guardian*, 2 October. www.theguardian.com/world/2012/oct/02/north-korea-defector-family-blackmail.

Hasisi, Badi, and David Weisburd. 2014. "Policing Terrorism and Police–Community relations: Views of the Arab Minority in Israel." *Police Practice and Research* 15/2: 158–172.

Hastings, Justin. 2016. *A Most Enterprising Country: North Korea in the Global Economy.* Cornell University Press.

Hirschman, Albert O. 1993. "Exit, Voice, and the Fate of the German Democratic Republic: An Essay in Conceptual History." *World Politics* 45/2:173–202.

Hockstader, Lee. 1996. "Who Killed Choi Duk Keun? North Korea's Hand Suspected in Slaying of Seoul Diplomat in Russia." *Washington Post*, 24 October.

Holland, Alisha, and Margaret Peters. 2020. "Explaining Migration Timing: Political Information and Opportunities." *International Organization* 74:560–583.

Hopkins, Valerie. 2021. "Pulling Levers in Exile, Belarus Opposition Leader Works to Keep Her Influence Alive." *New York Times*, 22 July. www.nytimes .com/2021/07/22/world/europe/belarus-opposition-svetlana-tikhanovskaya .html.

Hong, Christine. 2013. "Introduction to the Special Issue: Reframing North Korean Human Rights (Christine Hong and Hazel Smith, guest eds.)." *Critical Asian Studies* 45/4: 511–532.

Howard, Marc Morje. 2012. *The Weakness of Civil Society in Post-Communist Europe.* Cambridge University Press.

Hsu, Madeline. 2015. *The Good Immigrants: How the Yellow Peril Became the Model Minority.* Princeton University Press.

Hu, Elise. 2016. "South Korea's Newest TV Stars Are North Korean Defectors." NPR, 31 January. www.npr.org/sections/parallels/2016/01/31/ 464798910/south-koreas-newest-tv-stars-are-north-korean-defectors.

Hudson, John. 2019. "A Shadowy Group Trying to Overthrow Kim Jong Un Allegedly Raided a North Korean Embassy in Broad Daylight." *Washington Post*, 15 March. www.washingtonpost.com/world/national-security/a-shad owy-group-trying-to-overthrow-kim-jong-un-raided-a-north-korean-embassy-in-broad-daylight/2019/03/15/ae4208a4-c451-4886-b608-f5ac1f182d3d_story.html

Human Rights Watch. 2018. "Japan: Protect Victims Enticed to North Korea." 21 August. www.hrw.org/news/2018/08/21/japan-protect-victims-enticed-north-korea#.

Hundt, David, Jessica Walton, and Soo-Jung Elisha Lee. 2018. "Politics of Conditional Citizenship in South Korea." *Journal of Contemporary Asia* 49/3:434–451.

Hunter, Wendy. 2019. *Undocumented Nationals: Between Statelessness and Citizenship*. Cambridge University Press.

Hur, Aram. 2018. "Adapting to Democracy: National Identity and the Political Development of North Korean Defectors." *Journal of East Asian Studies*, 18/1:97-115.

Hur, Aram. 2020. "Refugee Perceptions toward Democratic Citizenship: A Narrative Analysis of North Koreans." *Comparative Politics* 52/3:473–493.

Ishikawa, M. 2018. *A River in Darkness: One Man's Escape from North Korea*. AmazonCrossing.

Ja Song Nam. 2014. "Letter Dated March 14 from the Permanent Representative of the Democratic People's Republic of Korea to the United Nations Addressed to the President of the Security Council." 14 March. S/2014/194.

Jang, Il Hun. 2014. "Ambassador Jang Il Hun on Human Rights in North Korea." Council on Foreign Relations, 20 October. www.cfr.org/event/ambassador-jang-il-hun-human-rights-north-korea-0.

Jeong, Andrew. 2018. "Hackers Steal Personal Information of North Korean Defectors in South Korea." *Wall Street Journal*, 28 December. www.wsj.com/articles/hackers-steal-personal-information-of-north-korean-defectors-in-south-korea-11546001022?mod=article_inline.

Jeong, Andrew. 2020. "North Korea Harasses Defectors with Calls, Texts: 'Are You Having Fun These Days?'" *Wall Street Journal*, 15 August, www.wsj.com/articles/north-korea-harasses-defectors-with-calls-texts-are-you-having-fun-these-days-11597492800.

Ji, Da-gyum. 2023. "Unification Ministry to Shift Focus to North Korean Human Rights." *Korea Herald*, 3 July. www.koreaherald.com/view.php?ud=20230703000762.

Jin, Changhao. 2015. "We Reveal, Once Again, the True Identity of the Human Trash, Sin Tong Hyok." YouTube, 12 March. www.youtube.com/watch?v=xbd4TqipHYk.

Jin, Dong Hyeok. 2013. "Re-defectors Scorn 'Society of Darkness.'" *Daily NK*, 1 October. www.dailynk.com/english/redefectors-scorn-society-of-darkn/.

Jolley, Mary Ann. 2014. "The Strange Tale of Yeonmi Park." *The Diplomat*, 10 December. https://thediplomat.com/2014/12/the-strange-tale-of-yeonmi-park/.

Joppke, Christian. 2005. *Selecting by Origin: Ethnic Migration in the Liberal State*. Harvard University Press.

Jung, Kyunga, Bronwen Dalton, and Jacqueline Willis. 2017. "The Onward Migration of North Korean Refugees to Australia: In Search of Cosmopolitan Habitus." *Cosmopolitan Civil Societies: An Interdisciplinary Journal* 9/3:1–20.

Jung, Won-Gi. 2021. "Just Two North Korean Defectors Reach South Korea from April to June." *NKNews*, 16 July. www.nknews.org/2021/07/just-two-north-korean-defectors-reach-south-korea-from-april-to-june/.

Kadhum, Oula. 2021. "Iraqi Diaspora Mobilization and the Future Development of Iraq." Atlantic Council, March. www.atlanticcouncil.org/in-depth-research-reports/iraqi-diaspora-mobilization-and-the-future-development-of-iraq/.

Kang, Mi Jin. 2014a. "Laos 9 Sent Home to Embody Kimist 'Generosity.'" *Daily NK*, 30 April. www.dailynk.com/english/laos-9-sent-home-to-embody-kimist/.

Kang, Mi Jin. 2014b. "More Footage of Repatriated Defectors from the 'Laos 9' Released." *DailyNK*, 15 December. www.dailynk.com/english/more-footage-of-repatriated-defect/.

Kapur, Devesh. 2014. "Political Effects of International Migration." *Annual Review of Political Science* 17:479–502.

Kasulis, Kelly. 2020. "North Korean Defector Arrested After Trying to Return to the DPRK." *NKNews*, 19 September. www.nknews.org/2020/09/north-korean-defector-arrested-after-attempting-to-cross-border-into-dprk/?t=1600669692477.

KBS World Radio. 2006. "Washington's Recent Acceptance of North Korean Defectors." 11 May. http://world.kbs.co.kr/english/program/program_korea today_detail.htm?No=85¤t_page=46.

KCNA. 2012a. "DPRK Woman Interviewed upon Her Return Home." 28 June. www.kcna.co.jp/item/2012/201206/news28/20120628-23ee.html, and www.kcna.co.jp/item/2012/201207/news02/20120702-13ee.html.

KCNA. 2012b. "'Defectors from North' Interviewed after Return to DPRK." 8 November. www.kcna.co.jp/item/2012/201211/news08/20121108-19ee.html.

KCNA. 2013a. "Round-Table Talks with Inhabitants Who Came Home." 30 September. www.kcna.co.jp/item/2013/201309/news30/20130930-26ee.html.

KCNA. 2013b. "Round-Table Talks Held with Inhabitants upon Their Return Home from S. Korea." 20 December. www.kcna.co.jp/item/2013/201312/news20/20131220-21ee.html.

KCNA. 2013c. "Round-Table Talks Held with Teenagers Who Came Back to DPRK." 20 June. www.kcna.co.jp/item/2013/201306/news20/20130620-20ee.html.

KCNA. 2013d. "Round-Table Talks Held with Inhabitants upon Their Return Home from South." 17 May. www.kcna.co.jp/item/2013/201305/news17/20130517-12ee.html.

KCNA. 2013e. "Traitor Jang Song Thaek Executed." *Korea Central News Agency*, 13 December. www.northkoreatech.org/2013/12/13/full-text-of-kcna-announcement-on-execution-of-jang/.

KCNA. 2014. "Korean Central News Agency Hits Commission of Inquiry Report." 30 April.

KCNA Watch. 2020. "17th Enlarged Meeting of Political Bureau and 5th Meeting of Executive Policy Council of 7th Central Committee of WPK Held." *Korean Central News Agency*, 26 August. https://kcnawatch.org/news tream/1598428858-653773355/17th-enlarged-meeting-of-political-bureau-and-5th-meeting-of-executive-policy-council-of-7th-central-committee-of-wpk-held/.

Keck, Margaret, and Kathryn Sikkink. 1998. *Activists Beyond Borders*. Cornell University Press.

Kim, Bumsoo. 2019. "Are North Korean Compatriots 'Korean'?" *Journal of Korean Studies* 24/1:149–171.

Kim Byung-yeon. 2017. *Unveiling the North Korean Economy: Collapse and Transition*. Cambridge University Press.

Kim, Eleana. 2010. *Adopted Territory: Transnational Korean Adoptees and the Politics of Belonging*. Duke University Press.

Kim Eun-joong. 2020. "U.S. Charges Kim Jong-nam Assassination 'Mastermind'." *Chosun Ilbo*, 14 September. https://english.chosun.com/site/data/html_dir/2020/09/14/2020091401633.html.

Kim, Hye-kyung. 2005. "The Korean Diaspora and Its Impact on Korean Development." *Asian & Pacific Migration Journal* 14/1:149–168.

Kim, Hyung-Jun. 2018. "Elderly Koreans Shut Out of Family Reunions Use Backchannels." *Associated Press*, 24 August. https://apnews.com/article/ap-top-news-north-korea-reunions-international-news-asia-pacific-38ce4edc552b4422ab75df43b60f3bf4.

Kim, Il Bong. 2012. "S. Korean Clan of Traitors Denounced for Allurement and Abduction of North Korean Citizens." *Pyongyang Times*, 30 June, pp. 6, 8.

Kim, In Ryong. 2016. "Kim In Ryong (DPRK) on Human Rights – Press Conference (13 December 2016)." UN Web TV video. http://webtv.un.org/watch/kim-in-ryong-dprk-on-human-rights-press-conference-13-december-2016/5246257589001/?term=&lan=original.

Kim, Jaeeun. 2016. *Contested Embrace: Transnational Border Politics in Twentieth-Century Korea*. Stanford University Press.

Kim, J. I. 2010. "A Study of the Roles of NGOs for North Korean Refugees' Human Rights." *Journal of Immigrant and Refugee Studies*, 8/1:76–90.

Kim, Jeongmin, and Nils Weisensee. 2021. "North Korean Hackers Breach Prominent Defector's Account in Targeted Hack." *NKNews*, 7 September.

www.nknews.org/2021/09/north-korean-hackers-breach-prominent-defect ors-accounts-in-targeted-attack/.

Kim, Mikyoung. 2012. *Securitization of Human Rights: North Korean Refugees in East Asia*. Praeger.

Kim, Mikyoung. 2013. "North Korean Refugees' Nostalgia: The Border People's Narratives." *Asian Politics and Policy* 5/4:523–542.

Kim, Min-Jung. 2021. "Is the South Korean Government Fiddling with an Idea for Prohibiting Radio Broadcasting to North Korea?" CSIS, 7 October. https://beyondparallel.csis.org/is-the-south-korean-government-fiddling-with-an-idea-for-prohibiting-radio-broadcasting-to-north-korea/.

Kim, Monica. 2019. *The Interrogation Rooms of the Korean War*. Princeton University Press.

Kim Myung-a. 2015. "How Does Diaspora Mobilization Become a Causal Feature of Structural Change?" *Journal of Asian Security and International Affairs* 2/3:266–290.

Kim, Myong-song. 2020. "N. Korean Spy Chief Demoted for Quarantine Failure." *Chosun Ilbo*, 29 September. http://english.chosun.com/site/data/html_dir/2020/09/29/2020092901840.html.

Kim, Nadia. 2008. *Imperial Citizens: Koreans and Race from Seoul to LA*. Stanford University Press.

Kim, Nora Hui-Jung. 2013. "Flexible Yet Inflexible: Development of Dual Citizenship in Korea." *Journal of Korean Studies* 18/1:7–28.

Kim, Nora Hui-Jung. 2016. "Naturalizing Korean Ethnicity and Making Ethnic Difference: Comparison of North Korean Settlement and Foreign Bride Incorporation Policies in South Korea." *Asian Ethnicity* 17/2:185–198.

Kim, Richard. 2011. *The Quest for Statehood: Korean Immigrant Nationalism and U.S. Sovereignty 1905–1945*. Oxford University Press.

Kim, Soo-am et al. 2017. *Study on North Korean Defectors' Perceptions about Democracy and the Market*. Korea Institute for National Unification.

Kim, Suk-young. 2014. *DMZ Crossing: Performing Emotional Citizenship along the Korean Border*. Columbia University Press.

Kim Suki. 2020. "The Underground Movement Trying to Topple the North Korean Regime." *New Yorker*, 23 November. www.newyorker.com/magazine/2020/11/23/the-underground-movement-trying-to-topple-the-north-korean-regime.

Kim, Tong-hyung. 2017. "Other Mysterious Deaths of North Korea's Perceived Enemies." *Associated Press*, 3 March. https://apnews.com/article/3397f5916d 7d478daea3da4c01703a38.

Kim, Victoria. 2019. "She Fled North Korea for a Better Life. How Her Lonely, Impoverished Death Became Political." *Los Angeles Times*, 9 September.

www.latimes.com/world-nation/story/2019-09-08/han-sung-ok-north-korea-refugee-death.

Kim, Yoo Jin. 2018. "Re-defectors to North Korea Give Internal Lectures on Defection Regret." *DailyNK*, 28 December. www.dailynk.com/english/39074-2/.

Kim, Yoon-Young. 2009. *Making National Subjects: Education and Adaptation among North Korean Immigrants in South Korea*. PhD dissertation, University of Hawai'i.

King, Robert. 2022. "In Significant Policy Shift, President Yoon Highlights North Korean Human Rights." Korea Economic Institute, 21 September. https://keia.org/the-peninsula/in-significant-policy-shift-president-yoon-highlights-north-korea-human-rights-issues/.

Kirby, Michael. 2014. "Exchange between Justice Kirby and DPRK Councillor Kim Song." 22 October. Clip from United Nations webcast, webtv.un.org, reposted on www.michaelkirby.com.au/content/epic-exchange-between-justice-kirby-and-dprk-councillor-kim-song-1.

Ko, Dong-hwan. 2016. "Cheong Wa Dae Accused of Votes Bid over N. Korean Defectors." *Korea Times*, April. www.koreatimes.co.kr/www/news/nation/2016/04/485_202314.html.

Koinova, M. 2009. "Diasporas and Democratization in the Post-Communist World." *Communist and Post-Communist Studies* 42/1:41–64.

Korea Times. 2010. "2 NK Spies Arrested in Plot to Kill Ranking Defector." 21 April. www.koreatimes.co.kr/www/nation/2023/10/113_64572.html.

Kwon, J. 2019. "She Fled North Korea for a Better Life. She Died With Her Young Son in an Apartment in Seoul." CNN, 12 September. www.cnn.com/2019/09/21/asia/north-korean-defector-funeral-intl-hnk/index.html.

Lankov, Andrei. 2006. "Bitter Taste of Paradise: North Korean Refugees in South Korea." *Journal of East Asian Studies* 6/1:105–137.

Lankov, Andrei. 2020. "Why North Koreans 'Double-Defect' to the DPRK after Risking It All to Run South." *NKNews*, 23 September. www.nknews.org/2020/09/why-north-koreans-double-defect-to-the-dprk-after-risking-it-all-to-run-south/.

Lankov, Andrei, In-ok Kwak, and Chong-Bin Cho. 2012. "Organizational Life: Daily Surveillance and Daily Resistance in North Korea." *Journal of East Asian Studies* 12/2:193–214.

Lee, Ahlam. 2016. *North Korean Defectors in a New and Competitive Society*. Lexington Press.

Lee, Chae-Un. 2021. "North Korea Continues to Erect Disease Control Stations at Local Markets, Police Stations." *DailyNK*, 13 January. www.dailynk.com/

english/north-korea-continues-erect-disease-control-stations-local-markets-police-stations/.

Lee, Chulwoo. 2010. "South Korea: Transformation of Citizenship and the State-Nation Nexus." *Journal of Contemporary Asia* 40/2:230–251.

Lee, Chulwoo. 2012. "How Can You Say You're Korean? Law, Governmentality and National Membership in South Korea." *Citizenship Studies* 16/1:85–102.

Lee, Sang Yong. 2013. "49 Spies: 21 Disguised as Defectors." *Daily NK*, 11 October. www.dailynk.com/english/read.php?cataId=nk00100& num=11069.

Lee, Sohoon, and Yi-Chun Chien. 2017. "The Making of 'Skilled' Overseas Koreans: Transformation of Visa Policies for Co-ethnic Migrants in South Korea." *Journal of Ethnic and Migration Studies* 43/10:2193–2210.

Len, Samuel. 2003. "Pyongyang Official Dies of Car Crash Injuries." *New York Times*, 28 October. www.nytimes.com/2003/10/28/news/pyongyang-official-dies-of-crash-injuries.html.

Levi, Nicolas. 2017. "The Community of North Korean Elites and Defectors in Eastern European Countries." Working paper, November.

Levitsky, Steven, and Lucan A. Way. 2010. *Competitive Authoritarianism: Hybrid Regimes after the Cold War*. Cambridge University Press.

Levitt, Peggy. 1998. "Social Remittances: Migration Driven Local-Level Forms of Cultural Diffusion." *International Migration Review* 32/4:926–948.

Lie, John. 2008. *Zainichi (Koreans in Japan): Diasporic Nationalism and Postcolonial Identity*. University of California Press.

Lie, John, ed. 2014. *Multiethnic Korea? Multiculturalism, Migration and Peoplehood Diversity in Contemporary South Korea*. University of California Press.

"Lie and Truth: Who Is Sin Dong Hyok?" 2014. 4 November. Uriminzokkiri video [Parts I and II], reposted to www.youtube.com/watch?v=P82aad 8QQW4.

Lim, Hyun-chin, and Young Chul Chung. 2006. "Political and Human Rights Issues Surrounding North Korean Defectors." *Review of Korean Studies* 9/ 1:87–116.

Lim Il and Adam Zulawnik. 2021. *Interviews With North Korean Defectors: From Kim Shin-Jo to Thae Yong-Ho*. Routledge.

Liu, Amy. 2021. *The Language of Political Incorporation: Chinese Migrants in Europe*. Temple University Press.

Lloyd, Lindsay. 2019. "Bush Institute Scholarship Helps North Korean Refugees Thrive." Bush Center, 21 June. www.bushcenter.org/publications/ articles/2019/6/scholarship-helps-refugees-thrive.html.

Loxton, James, and Timothy Power. 2021. "Introducing Authoritarian Diasporas: Causes and Consequences of Authoritarian Elite Dispersion." *Democratization* 8/3:465-483.

Mackinnon, Mark. 2010. "North Korean Defectors Want to Liberate Former Home." *Globe and Mail*, 17 December. www.theglobeandmail.com/news/world/north-korean-defectors-want-to-liberate-former-home/article1320350/.

Madokoro, Laura. 2016. *Elusive Refuge: Chinese Migrants in the Cold War.* Harvard University Press.

Mahmoud, Toman Omar, Hillel Rapoport, Andreas Steinmayr, and Christoph Trebesch. 2017. "The Effect of Labor Migration on the Diffusion of Democracy: Evidence from a Former Soviet Republic." *American Economic Journal: Applied Economics* 9/3:36–69.

Marsh, Sarah. 2021. "The Facebook Group that Triggered Cuba's First Wave of Protests." *Reuters*, 9 August. www.reuters.com/world/americas/facebook-group-that-staged-first-cubas-wave-protests-2021-08-09/.

Marshall, T. H. 1964. *Citizenship and Social Class.* Cambridge University Press.

McCurry, Justin. 2014. "The Defector Who Wants to Go Back to North Korea." *Guardian*, 22 April. www.theguardian.com/world/2014/apr/22/defector-wants-to-go-back-north-korea.

Menon, Praveen, and Emily Chow. 2017. "Murder at the Airport: The Brazen Attack on N.Korean Leader's Half-Brother." *Reuters*, 16 February. www.reuters.com/article/uk-northkorea-malaysia-kim-murder/murder-at-the-airport-the-brazen-attack-on-north-korean-leaders-half-brother-idUKKBN15V1AS.

Miller, Michael, and Margaret Peters. 2020. "Restraining the Huddled Masses: Migration Policy and Autocratic Survival." *British Journal of Political Science* 50/2:403–433.

Miyoshi-Jager, Sheila. 2003. *Narratives of Nation-Building in Korea.* M.E. Sharpe.

Morris, Andrew. 2022. *Defectors from the PRC to Taiwan, 1960–1989.* Routledge.

Morris-Suzuki, Tessa. 2007. *Exodus to North Korea: Shadows from Japan's Cold War.* Rowman & Littlefield.

Moss, Dana M. 2020. "Voice after Exit: Explaining Diaspora Mobilization for the Arab Spring." *Social Forces* 98/4:1669–1694.

Moss, Dana M. 2021. *The Arab Spring Abroad: Diaspora Activism Against Authoritarian Regimes.* Cambridge University Press.

Muller-Funk, Lea. 2019. *Egyptian Diaspora Activism during the Arab Uprisings: Insights from Paris and Vienna.* Routledge.

Mylonas, Harris. 2013. "Politics of Diaspora Management in the Republic of Korea." *The Asan Institute for Policy Studies Issue Brief 81*:1–12.

Nanes, Matthew J. 2020. "Policing in Divided Societies." *Conflict Management and Peace Science* 37/5:580–604.

Nasr, Mary. 2014. "(Ethnic) Nationalism in North Korean Political Ideology and Culture." PhD dissertation, University of Sydney.

Nedelcu, Mihaela. 2019. "Digital Diasporas." In *Routledge Handbook of Diaspora Studies* (Robin Cohen and Carolin Fischer, eds.; Routledge), pp. 241–250.

New York Times. 2002. "Defector Who Returned to North Korea Escapes Again to Seoul." 14 February. www.nytimes.com/2002/02/14/world/ defector-who-returned-to-north-korea-escapes-again-to-seoul.html.

Nugent, Elizabeth, and Alexandra Siegel. 2023. "#Activism from Exile: How Exiles Mobilized Large-Scale Protests in Egypt." Working paper.

Ozden, Çağlar, Christopher R. Parsons, Maurice Schiff, and Terrie L. Walmsley. 2011. "Where on Earth Is Everybody: The Evolution of Global Bilateral Migration 1960–2000." *World Bank Economic Review* 25/1:12–56. https:// elibrary.worldbank.org/doi/10.1093/wber/lhr024.

Panagiotidis, Jannis. 2015. "What Is the German's Fatherland? The GDR and Resettlement of Ethnic Germans from Socialist Countries (1949–1989)." *East European Politics & Societies* 29/1:120–146.

Park, Alyssa. 2019. *Sovereignty Experiments: Korean Migrants and the Building of Borders in Northeast Asia, 1860–1945*. Cornell University Press.

Park Chan-kyoung. 2011. "Seoul Arrests Suspected N. Korean Assassin." *Agence France-Presse*, 16 September.

Park Han-na. 2019. "Group Claims Establishment of North Korean Provisional Government." *Korea Herald*, 1 March. www.koreaherald.com/view.php? ud=20190301000072.

Park, Hien Ju. 2011. *Twice Illegal: Ethnic Community, Identity and Social Networks among the North Korean Defectors in the U.S.* PhD dissertation, University of California–Irvine.

Park, Hyung Ok. 2015. *The Capitalist Unconscious: From Korean Unification to Transnational Korea*. Columbia University Press.

Park, Jihyun, and Seh-Lynn Chai. 2023. *The Hard Road Out: One Woman's Escape from North Korea*. HarperNorth.

Park, Joowon. 2023. *Belonging in a House Divided*. University of California Press.

Park, Ju-min. 2013. "North Korea's Kim Tries New Tack with Defectors: Being Nice." Reuters, 18 August. www.reuters.com/article/2013/08/19/us-korea-north-defectors-insight-idUSBRE97H0D120130819.

Park, Jung-Sun, and Paul Chang. 2005. "Contention in the Construction of a Global Korean Community: The Overseas Korean Act." *Journal of Korean Studies* 10/1:1–27.

Park, Lisa Sun-Hee. 2005. *Consuming Citizenship: Children of Asian Immigrant Entrepreneurs*. Stanford University Press.

Park, M. K., et al. 2013. *Tongil Usik Chosa* [Survey on Perceptions of Unification]. Seoul National University.

Park, Seong Guk. 2013. "Ha: Kim and Family Are South Korean Citizens." *Daily NK*, 16 July. www.dailynk.com/english/read.php?num=10743&cataId=nk00100.

Park, Yeonmi (with Maryanne Vollers). 2015. *In Order to Live*. Penguin Press.

Park, Young Hwan. 2013. "Ministry of Foreign Affairs Has Established an 'International Cooperation Team for the Ethnic Community,' Which Will Be Dedicated to Defectors." *Newsis*, 29 August. www.newsis.com/view?id=NISX20130828_0012317130.

Perry, Elizabeth. 2008. "Chinese Conceptions of Rights." *Perspectives on Politics* 6/1:37–50.

Peters, Margaret. 2017. *Trading Barriers: Immigration and the Remaking of Globalization*. Princeton University Press.

Peterson, Glenn. 2008. "To Be or Not Be a Refugee: The International Politics of the Hong Kong Refugee Crisis, 1949–55." *Journal of Imperial and Commonwealth History* 36/2.171–193.

Pop-Eleches, Grigore, and Joshua Tucker. 2017. *Communism's Shadow: Historical Legacies and Contemporary Political Attitudes*. Princeton University Press.

Power, John. 2014. "North Korea: Defectors and their Skeptics." *The Diplomat*, 29 October. https://thediplomat.com/2014/10/north-korea-defectors-and-their-skeptics/.

Power, John. 2015. "Why Are North Korean Defectors Being Turned Away in Europe?" *The Diplomat*, 17 June. https://thediplomat.com/2015/06/why-are-north-korean-defectors-being-turned-away-in-europe/.

Radio Free Asia. 2019. "Survey: North Korean Defectors Fared Better Economically Last Year." 25 April. www.rfa.org/english/news/korea/nk-defector-stats-2018-04252019101211.html.

Radio Free Asia. 2021. "North Korean Phone Brokers Take Huge Risk to Resume Remittances." 30 August. www.rfa.org/english/news/korea/broker-08302021191858.html.

Ragazzi, Francesco. 2009. "Governing Diasporas." *International Political Sociology* 3/4:378–397.

Ragazzi, Francesco. 2012. "Diaspora: The Politics of Its Meanings." *International Political Sociology* 6/1:107–111.

Rauhala, Emily. 2015. "North Korean Camp Survivor Admits He Was Not Straight About His Story." *Time*, 19 January. https://time.com/3673272/north-korean-camp-survivor/.

Rhee, Kyung-ha. 2021. "캐나다 "탈북민 수용, 한국이 항구적 해결책 [Canada: South Korea is a Permanent Solution for North Korean Defectors]." Radio Free Asia, 28 October. www.rfa.org/korean/in_focus/human_rights_defector-10282021144134.html.

Rothwell, James. 2016. "North Korean Defector Returns Home After 16 Years, Rips Up Her Memoirs on Camera." *Telegraph*, 21 January. www.telegraph.co.uk/news/worldnews/asia/northkorea/12112246/North-Korean-defector-returns-home-after-16-years-and-rips-up-her-memoirs-on-camera.html.

Ryall, Julian. 2017. "Defector 'Shocked' She Might Have Aided Assassination of Pastor Helping North Koreans Flee the Regime." *Telegraph*, 25 July. www.telegraph.co.uk/news/2017/07/25/defector-shocked-might-have-aided-assassination-pastor-aiding/.

Ryang, Sonia. 1997. *North Koreans in Japan: Language, Ideology, and Identity*. Westview Press.

Ryang, Sonia. 2016. "The Rise and Fall of Chongryun: From Chosenjin to Zainichi and Beyond." *The Asia-Pacific Journal* 14/15:1–16. https://apjjf.org/2016/15/Ryang.html.

Ryang, Sonia, and John Lie, eds. 2009. *Diaspora Without Homeland: Being Korean in Japan*. University of California Press.

Safran, William. 1991. "Diasporas in Modern Societies: Myths of Homeland and Return." *Diaspora: a Journal of Transnational Studies* 1/1:83–99.

Scarlatoiu, Greg, Jana Johnson, and Miran Song. 2013. "Redefectors to North Korea: Exaggeration or the Beginning of a Trend?" *NKNews*, 24 January. www.hrnkinsider.org/2013/01/re-defection-to-north-korea.html.

Schmitter, Philippe, and Terry Karl. 1991. "What Democracy Is . . . and Is Not." *Journal of Democracy* 2/3: 75–88.

Schwarzman, Nathan. 2008. "Fraudulent NK Defectors to Be Expelled from the UK." *Asian Correspondent*, 29 July. https://asiancorrespondent.com/2008/07/fraudulent-north-korean-defectors-to-be-expelled-from-uk/#LLJvb23tbRxvy1SY.97.

Seol, Dong-hoon, and John Skrenty. 2009. "Ethnic Return Migration and Hierarchical Nationhood: Korean Chinese Foreign Workers in South Korea." *Ethnicities* 9/2:147–174.

Shain, Yossi. 1999. *Marketing the American Creed Abroad: Diasporas in the US and Their Homelands*. Cambridge University Press.

Shain, Yossi. 2010. *The Frontier of Loyalty: Political Exiles in the Age of the Nation-state*. University of Michigan Press.

Shain, Yossi, and Aharon Barth. 2003. "Diasporas and International Relations Theory." *International Organization* 57/3:449–479.

Shim, Elizabeth. 2015. "Human Rights Watch: Border Control, Surveillance Tightened Under Kim Jong Un." *UPI*, 2 September. www.upi.com/Top_News/World-News/2015/09/02/Human-Rights-Watch-Border-control-surveillance-increased-under-Kim-Jong-Un/2321441219387/.

Shin, Dong Hyuk (with Blaine Harden). 2012. *Escape from Camp 14*. Viking/Penguin.

Shin, Gi-Wook. 2006. *Ethnic Nationalism in Korea*. Stanford University Press.

Shipper, Apichai. 2010. "Nationalisms of and Against Zainichi Koreans in Japan." *Asian Politics and Policy* 2/1: 55–75.

Shorrock, Timothy. 2019. "Did the CIA Orchestrate an Attack on the North Korean Embassy in Spain?" *The Nation*. 2 May. www.thenation.com/article/archive/did-the-cia-orchestrate-an-attackon-the-north-korean-embassy-spain-cia/.

Smith, Josh, and Hyonhee Shin. 2019. "'A Target on the Back': North Korea Embassy Raid Thrusts Shadowy Group into Spotlight." *Reuters*, 27 March. www.reuters.com/article/uk-spain-northkorea-group/a-target-on-the-back-north-korea-embassy-raid-thrusts-shadowy-group-into-the-spotlight-idUSKCN1R817K?il=0.

Sobel, Andrew. 2016. *Citizenship as Foundation of Rights*. Cambridge University Press.

Sohn, Ae-Lee, and Nae-Young Lee. 2012. "A Study on the Attitude of South Koreans toward North Korean Defectors: National Identity and Multi-Cultural Acceptability." *Journal of Asia-Pacific Studies* 19/3:5–34.

Son, Sarah. 2016. "Identity, Security, and the Nation: Understanding the South Korean Response to North Korean Defectors." *Asian Ethnicity* 17/2:171–184.

Song, Gae-Hee. 2012. *North Korean Migrant Integration into South Korean Society*. PhD dissertation, Syracuse University.

Song, Jay. 2013. "'Smuggled Refugees': North Korean Irregular Migration to China and Southeast Asia." *International Migration* 51/4:158–173.

Song, Jay. 2015. "Twenty Years' Evolution of North Korean Migration, 1994–2014: A Human Security Perspective." *Asia and the Pacific Policy Studies* 2/2:399–441.

Song, Jay, and Steven Denney. 2019. "Studying North Korea through North Korean Migrants: Lessons from the Field." *Critical Asian Studies* 51/3:451–466.

Song, Jiyoung. 2015. "Why Do North Korean Defectors' Testimonies So Often Fall Apart?" *Guardian*, 13 October. www.theguardian.com/world/2015/oct/13/why-do-north-korean-defector-testimonies-so-often-fall-apart.

Song, Jiyong, and Markus Bell. 2019. "North Korean Secondary Migration to the UK." *Migration Studies* 7/2: 160–179.

Stanton, Joshua. 2016. "Who Killed Pastor Han Chung-ryeol?" *One Free Korea* (blog), 3 May. https://freekorea.us/2016/05/who-killed-pastor-han-chung-ryeol.

Suh, You Kyung. n.d. "Some Problems of South Korean Government's Current Integrating Policies Regarding North Korean Defectors and Its Future Options." Kyunghee University.

Sunwoo, Carla. 2014. "Young Defectors Often Regret Leaving the North." *Joongang Ilbo*, 30 July. https://koreajoongangdaily.joins.com/2014/07/29/features/Young-defectors-often-regret-leaving-the-North/2992719.html.

Tansey, Oisin. 2016. *The International Politics of Authoritarian Rule*. Oxford University Press.

Tarrow, Sidney. 2005. *The New Transnational Activism*. Cambridge University Press.

Tsourapas, Gerasimos. 2018. "Authoritarian Emigration States: Soft Power and Cross-Border Mobility in the Middle East." *International Political Science Review* 39/3:400–416.

Tsourapas, Gerasimos. 2021. "Global Autocracies: Strategies of Transnational Repression, Legitimation, & Co-Optation in World Politics." *International Studies Review* 23/3:616–644.

Tsuda, Takeyuki, and Changzoo Song. 2019. *Diasporic Returns to the Ethnic Homeland: The Korean Diaspora in Comparative Perspective*. Palgrave Macmillan.

United Nations, Commission of Inquiry on Human Rights in the Democratic People's Republic of Korea [UNCOI]. 2014. *Report of the Commission of Inquiry on Human Rights in the Democratic People's Republic of Korea.* www.ohchr.org/en/hr-bodies/hrc/co-idprk/commission-inquiryon-h-rin-dprk/.

UN Web TV. 2014. "ID Commission of Inquiry on DPRK – 31st Meeting 25th Regular Session of Human Rights Council." 17 March. http://webtv.un.org/meetings-events/general-assembly/general-debate/71st-session-%255Ball-languages%255D/watch/id-commission-of-inquiry-on-dprk-31st-meeting-25th-regular-session-of-human-rights-council/3350537719001?page=171.

UniKorea Blog. 2017. "또 다른 통일의 시작, 제3국 출생 청소년 [Start of Another Unification, Youth Born in Third Countries]." 13 March. unikorea blog.tistory.com/6913.

Vasanthakumar, Ashwini. 2022. *The Ethics of Exile: A Political Theory of Diaspora*. Oxford University Press.

Vertovec, Steven. 2009. *Transnationalism*. Routledge.

Voice of America. 2021. "미국 내 탈북민들 "북한 최장 국경 봉쇄로 간부들도 경제난 ... 주민들 삶 간섭만 안 해도 감사할 것 [North Korean Defectors in US: Sanctions Lead to Hardship for Elites]." 11 November. www.voakorea.com/a/6308253.html.

Vollers, Maryanne. 2015. "The Woman Who Faces the Wrath of North Korea." *Guardian*, 15 March. www.theguardian.com/world/2015/mar/15/park-yeon-mi-north-korea-defector.

Wan, Ming. 2003. "Tensions in Recent Sino-Japanese Relations: The May 2002 Shenyang Incident." *Asian Survey* 43/5: 826–844.

Watson, Iain. 2015. "The Korean Diaspora and Belonging in the UK: Identity Tensions Between North and South Koreans." *Social Identities* 21/6:545–561.

Weiser, Martin. 2021. "North Korea's Mistranslated Shoot-to-Kill Border Protection Order." East Asia Forum, 27 February. www.eastasiaforum.org/2021/02/27/north-koreas-mistranslated-shoot-to-kill-border-protection-order/.

Windrem, Robert, Ken Dilanian, and Abigail Williams. 2017. "North Korea Has a History of Assassination Attempts on Foreign Soil." NBC News, 21 November. www.nbcnews.com/news/north-korea/north-korea-has-history-assassination-attempts-foreign-soil-n823016.

Wolman, Andrew. 2014. "The South Korean Citizenship of North Korean Escapees in Law and Practice." *KLRI Journal of Law and Legislation* 4/2:225–253.

Yamaguchi, Mari. 2021. "Japan Court Summons N.Korean Leader Over Repatriation Program." *Associated Press*, 7 September. https://apnews.com/article/japan-discrimination-race-and-ethnicity-racial-injustice-north-korea-9b7c7ac2009185097dc0293e8568e285.

Yang, Dominic Meng-Hsuan. 2014. "Humanitarian Assistance and Propaganda War: Repatriation and Relief of the Nationalist Refugees in Hong Kong's Rennie's Mill Camp, 1950–55." *Journal of Chinese Overseas* 10/2:165–196.

Yang, Dominic Meng-Hsuan. 2021. *The Great Exodus from China: Trauma, Memory, and Identity in Modern Taiwan*. Cambridge University Press.

Ye, Min. 2014. *Diasporas and Foreign Direct Investment in China and India*. Cambridge University Press.

Yeo, Andrew, and Danielle Chubb, eds. 2018. *North Korean Human Rights: Activists and Networks*. Cambridge University Press.

Yonhap. 2014a. "S. Korea Reforming N. Korean Defector Interrogation System." 28 July. https://en.yna.co.kr/view/AEN20140728007800315.

Yonhap. 2014b. "Gukjeongwon, talbukja josasil gaebanghyeong bakkwo, ingwon bohogwan immyeong" [At the NIS, the North Korean Defectors'

Investigation Office Will Be Replaced, Human Rights Protection Officer Appointed]. 28 July. www.yna.co.kr/view/AKR20140728134500043.

Yonhap. 2021. "N.Korean Spy Indicted After Allegedly Working to Return Defectors Home." 10 November. https://en.yna.co.kr/view/AEN2021111 0004400315.

Yoon, Dasl. 2023. "China Appears to Have Repatriated North Koreans Despite International Pressure." *Wall Street Journal,* 13 October. www.wsj.com/world/asia/china-appears-to-have-repatriated-north-koreans-despite-international-pressure-3b0e99df.

Yoon, In Jin. 2001. "North Korean Diaspora: North Korean Defectors Abroad and in South Korea." *Development and Society* 3/1:1–26.

Yoon, In Jin. 2012. "Migration and the Korean Diaspora: A Comparative Description of Five Cases." *Journal of Ethnic and Migration Studies* 38/3:413–435.

Yoon, Jennifer. 2018. "'A Cage without Walls': Once in South Korea, North Koreans Have Little Chance of Getting Asylum Elsewhere." CBC News, 9 September. www.cbc.ca/news/canada/north-korea-defectors-canada-1.4785235.

Young, Benjamin. 2021. *Guns, Guerillas, and the Great Leader: North Korea and the Third World.* Stanford University Press.

Young, Leslie. 2017. "North Korean Defectors in Toronto Worried They May Be Deported." *Global News Canada*, 30 November. https://globalnews.ca/news/3890370/north-korean-defectors-in-toronto-worried-they-may-be-deported-they-treat-us-like-garbage/.

Zolkepli, Farik. 2020. "Feature: The Assassination of Kim Jong-nam." *ANN Asia News Network*, 13 February.

Zvobgo, Kelebogile. 2020. "Demanding Truth: The Global Transitional Justice Network and the Creation of Truth Commissions." *International Studies Quarterly* 64/3:609–625.

Acknowledgments

In 2008, I stood in a park overlooking the China–North Korea border, speaking with a woman who, though a Chinese citizen, had grown up in North Korea and frequently traveled back for work. "You and I are free," she said, pointing across the river. "People in North Korea are not." It was jarring to hear the United States and China grouped together as "free" places, but her comment lingered. Over the course of subsequent years of research, as I spoke with people who'd escaped North Korea, I grew interested not just in what they'd left behind, but the new lives they were building. How did people who'd grown up in one of the world's most restrictive autocracies perceive citizenship in a democracy? Given the choice, what kinds of political engagement did they find meaningful?

It takes immense courage to answer these questions, whether in the form of the written word, a story told aloud, or simply a life lived day by day. I extend my deepest gratitude to those who shared their answers. Only a small fraction of their insight appears here; I hope that the world recognizes how much they have to teach.

It took over a decade after that conversation in Dandong for those ideas to coalesce into a book. I began writing as an assistant professor at the University of Missouri and finished the manuscript at the University of Texas at Austin. I'm grateful to my Mizzou colleagues for providing an ideal junior faculty work environment, and a haven of normalcy, stability, and support. At UT, colleagues at the LBJ School, the Strauss and Clements Centers, the Government Department, and the Center for East Asian Studies have welcomed me into a collegial intellectual community. I'm especially grateful to Will Inboden and Bobby Chesney for bringing me to UT, enabling me not just to grow professionally, but to build a life for my family.

I'm grateful to hosts and participants in various fora whose feedback improved this work: the East Asia Institute; Stanford's Freeman Spogli Institute and Asia–Pacific Research Center; the Harvard Academy for International and Area Studies & Weatherhead Center; Notre Dame's Liu Institute; Washington University in St. Louis; the Institutes for Korean Studies at George Washington University and Indiana University; and panels at the 2016 and 2018 Association for Asian Studies conferences. I thank Adrian Buzo, Celeste Arrington, Patricia Goedde, and Jisoo Kim, who edited volumes and journal issues in which my early intellectual inquiries appeared. Sara Goodman, Aram Hur, and Amy Liu shared survey questions on citizenship and political incorporation. Series editors Benjamin Read, Mary Alice Haddad, and Erin Aeran Chung provided feedback that adduced additional thoroughness and clarity.

The Laboratory Program for Korean Studies of the ROK Ministry of Education and Korean Studies Promotion Service of the Academy of Korean Studies (AKS-2016-LAB-2250001) provided generous financial support. Victor Cha and the CSIS Korea Chair team offered a robust intellectual community and much helpful feedback. This project would not have been feasible without the organizations that circulated this survey; I'm grateful to them, and to every individual who shared a portion of their experience with me over the course of the past fifteen years. I thank Edward Goldring, Yujin Julia Jung, Brian Kim, Jeune Kim, Yu Bin Kim, Myunghee Lee, Joseph Lenox, Liz Newsom, Ken Nienhuser, and Eunbi Yu for research assistance, and Aram Hur, Andrew Yeo, and Steven Denney for ongoing dialogue.

None of this work would've been possible without the love and support of my family and friends, to whom I extend heartfelt gratitude. My final thanks go to my two sons, Joshua and Jacob, without whom this Element would've been finished years earlier, but with much less joy and meaning. This book is dedicated to them.

Politics and Society in East Asia

Erin Aeran Chung

The Johns Hopkins University

Erin Aeran Chung is the Charles D. Miller Professor of East Asian Politics in the Department of Political Science at the Johns Hopkins University. She specializes in East Asian political economy, migration and citizenship, and comparative racial politics. She is the author of *Immigration and Citizenship in Japan* (Cambridge, 2010, 2014; Japanese translation, Akashi Shoten, 2012) and *Immigrant Incorporation in East Asian Democracies* (Cambridge, 2020). Her research has been supported by grants from the Academy of Korean Studies, the Japan Foundation, the Japan Foundation Center for Global Partnership, the Social Science Research Council, and the American Council of Learned Societies.

Mary Alice Haddad

Wesleyan University

Mary Alice Haddad is the John E. Andrus Professor of Government, East Asian Studies, and Environmental Studies at Wesleyan University. Her research focuses on democracy, civil society, and environmental politics in East Asia as well as city diplomacy around the globe. A Fulbright and Harvard Academy scholar, Haddad is author of *Effective Advocacy: Lessons from East Asia's Environmentalists* (MIT, 2021), *Building Democracy in Japan* (Cambridge, 2012), and *Politics and Volunteering in Japan* (Cambridge, 2007), and co-editor of *Greening East Asia* (University of Washington, 2021), and *NIMBY Is Beautiful* (Berghahn Books, 2015). She has published in journals such as *Comparative Political Studies, Democratization, Journal of Asian Studies*, and *Nonprofit and Voluntary Sector Quarterly*, with writing for the public appearing in the *Asahi Shimbun, The Hartford Courant*, and the *South China Morning Post*.

Benjamin L. Read

University of California, Santa Cruz

Benjamin L. Read is a professor of Politics at the University of California, Santa Cruz. His research has focused on local politics in China and Taiwan, and he also writes about issues and techniques in comparison and field research. He is author of *Roots of the State: Neighborhood Organization and Social Networks in Beijing and Taipei* (Stanford, 2012), coauthor of *Field Research in Political Science: Practices and Principles* (Cambridge, 2015), and co-editor of *Local Organizations and Urban Governance in East and Southeast Asia: Straddling State and Society* (Routledge, 2009). His work has appeared in journals such as *Comparative Political Studies, Comparative Politics, The Journal of Conflict Resolution, The China Journal, The China Quarterly*, and *The Washington Quarterly*, as well as several edited books.

About the Series

The Cambridge Elements series on Politics and Society in East Asia offers original, multidisciplinary contributions on enduring and emerging issues in the dynamic region of East Asia by leading scholars in the field. Suitable for general readers and specialists alike, these short, peer-reviewed volumes examine common challenges and patterns within the region while identifying key differences between countries. The series consists of two types of contributions: (1) authoritative field surveys of established concepts and themes that offer roadmaps for further research; and (2) new research on emerging issues that challenge conventional understandings of East Asian politics and society. Whether focusing on an individual country or spanning the region, the contributions in this series connect regional trends with points of theoretical debate in the social sciences and will stimulate productive interchanges among students, researchers, and practitioners alike.

Cambridge Elements ᵔ

Politics and Society in East Asia

A full series listing is available at: www.cambridge.org/EPEA

Printed in the United States
by Baker & Taylor Publisher Services